THE END OF
CONVERSATION

Recent Titles in
Contributions in Sociology

The Underside of High-Tech: Technology and the Deformation of
Human Sensibilities
John W. Murphy, Algis Mickunas, and Joseph J. Pilotta, editors

Five Scenarios for the Year 2000
Franco Ferrarotti

Uniforms and Nonuniforms: Communication Through Clothing
Nathan Joseph

Housing Markets and Policies under Fiscal Austerity
Willem van Vliet—, editor

Religious Sociology: Interfaces and Boundaries
William H. Swatos, Jr., editor

Bureaucracy Against Democracy and Socialism
*Ronald M. Glassman, William H. Swatos, Jr., and Paul L. Rosen,
editors*

Housing and Neighborhoods: Theoretical and Empirical
Contributions
*Willem van Vliet—, Harvey Choldin, William Michelson, and David
Popenoe, editors*

The Mythmakers: Intellectuals and the Intelligentsia in Perspective
Raj P. Mohan, editor

The Organization-Society Nexus: A Critical Review of Models and
Metaphors
Ronald Corwin

The Concept of Social Structure
Douglas V. Porpora

Emile Durkheim: Ethics and the Sociology of Morals
Robert T. Hall

The Development of a Postmodern Self: A Computer-Assisted
Comparative Analysis of Personal Documents
Michael Wood and Louis Zurcher

FRANCO FERRAROTTI

THE END OF CONVERSATION

The Impact of Mass Media on Modern Society

Contributions in Sociology, Number 71

Greenwood Press

NEW YORK

WESTPORT, CONNECTICUT

LONDON

Library of Congress Cataloging-in-Publication Data

Ferrarotti, Franco.
  The end of conversation : the impact of mass media on modern
society / Franco Ferrarotti.
     p. cm.—(Contributions in sociology, ISSN 0084-9278 ; no.
71)
  Bibliography: p.
  Includes index.
  ISBN 0-313-26087-7 (lib. bdg. : alk. paper)
  1. Mass media—Social aspects. 2. Mass society. 3. Oral history.
4. Interpersonal communication. 5. Social history—Historiography.
6. Social sciences and history. I. Title. II. Series.
HM258.F47   1988
302.2′34—dc19   87-24966

British Library Cataloguing in Publication Data is available.

Library of Congress Catalog Card Number: 87-24966
ISBN: 0-313-26087-7
ISSN: 0084-9278

First published in 1988

Greenwood Press, Inc.
88 Post Road West, Westport, Connecticut 06881

Printed in the United States of America

The paper used in this book complies with the
Permanent Paper Standard issued by the National
Information Standards Organization (Z39.48-1984).

10 9 8 7 6 5 4 3 2 1

Contents

Preface

This book has appeared in Italian under the title *La storia e il quotidiano* (History and Everyday Life). The present American edition's title appropriately emphasizes the problem of the impact of mass media on present day society. The controversy between classical humanism and mass media is still open. Only a dogmatic approach could consider it solvable once and for all in terms of catastrophic opposition or uncritical integration. It seems clear that in the current Gutenberg-electronic reality, the relations between the various means of communication and information simultaneously present cannot be reduced to simple, radical alternatives. Rather, they require a much more flexible view of their respective, and often complementary, functions. The process of interaction between the media and their exploiters requires a deeper analysis of all the elements that mark them out, as each new medium is the mold of institutional developments, popular reactions and cultural contents of conflicting forces and tendencies which collide and evolve through time, giving rise continually to their opposites. The updating of the problems of information in the current situation of electronic pre-literacy cannot long be postponed in the name of a perennial, insurmountable Gutenbergian humanism. If we bear in mind the great shift occurring over the last several decades in studies on orality or literacy, which have also helped to give a new historical dimension to the current debate on the media, we become aware of our delay in learning the lesson originating in the research by Milton Parry half a century ago, and from the seminal insight of Harold Innis and the "Toronto School." These have more recently been followed by the work of Havelock and Watt on the consequences of literacy, taken up today by Harvey Graff. Much ground remains to be covered. Social and biological rhythms, as well as the social use of time and its perception by individuals and groups in particular historical contexts, are to be explored.

THE END OF CONVERSATION

1

The Interrupted
Conversation

BETWEEN TWO VOIDS

We have lost the everyday, and no longer have history. We live suspended between two voids. This loss has occurred at the very moment when we need to have the everyday transformed into history, so that history may be the history of everyone. In the next decades, a situation will become clear that today can be glimpsed only vaguely, in outline, almost mistily, making one think of the landscape of a foggy autumnal plain a drowsy traveller watches, on and off, from the window of a passing train, and which tends to dissolve into a clotted, milky stain. We have lost the ability to relate an experience in an orderly, expressive way. For reasons which are still rather mysterious, we have been abandoned by the art of storytelling. The thread of the story has been snapped. Narrative seems unexpectedly to have become superfluous. What remains is, by any standard, tedious and too slow for a world with bad nerves. As though a complex sentence were food too rich for average taste or a normal stomach, no one seems able any longer to savour, literally to digest, a sentence well composed from the grammatical and syntactical point of view, with, perhaps, a clause dependent on a dependent clause, a handful of relative pronouns, subjunctives, colons, and commas. Delicate stomachs predominate, so that we observe intelligences paying for their swiftness with scanty endurance and a good helping of sparkling superficiality. Telling a story is monotonous. It is tiring. It requires time, a taste for details, sharpness of sight, patience in describing the scene, a nose for dark corners and byways, a sense of touch, openness and availability to what is new and unexpected. These are qualities antithetical to the technological imperatives of a mass society and the mental habits prevailing in an age dominated by instantaneous images, unable to cope with meaningful discontinuities.

The image gives the illusion of the instant, global meaning; it is the definitive contraction of a whole story into a sign. Undoubtedly, the image, especially in photography, can perform a useful, deserving function of initial stimulus. However, there is a basic reservation to bear in mind. I tried to expound this in my *Dal documento alla testimonianza* (From document to evidence), concentrating on photography in the social sciences. Photography is the cyclops' eye. But Odysseus is the human reality, fleeing, clutching the goat's fleece. The cyclops shouts, grabs, grasps, pitiless and all-embracing. His eye is enormous, like an all-seeing—and also blind—wide-angle lens. Human reality does not lie in the photograph. As human reality is meaning, the making concrete, the construction of congealed meanings, it cannot be found in photography, but in the intention of the photographer. If there is no intention, the meaning too lapses—the selective criterion, the developing fact, the determining variable. Only the gesture, the click, remains, too easy not to appear stupid, not to be the conditioned reflex of mass, Sunday-best happiness which can't bear the idea of its own historical liquidation. To photograph means "to write with light": to write, or signify, mark, distribute light on reality so that it strikes with different intensity the stony datum of the everyday, bringing contrast to life. To write with light means in the first instance to need the dark, to summon up the shadows.

However, one fact seems certain. The flood of images which now flows out every day on a global scale tends to deprive the image of its value as basic evidence. We shall have to start thinking that in the beginning there was not the word but rather the image. The mass media are covering and flattening the world. Often, investigative journalism arrives before scientific analysis, weighted down with its own technical research apparatus. With great precision it catches the effect of "sameness," that is, of identity produced by the mass media, over and above the specific aspect of time and space, to the point of cancelling out historical variation and the circumstantial, or historically rooted, meaning of human experience. Once it was the gas stations, the same everywhere, in Arizona or the Po Valley, Provence or the suburbs of Chicago, an exact reflection of the global network of the oil multinations. Now, it is the shopping malls, those commercial pedestrian precincts, which are, moreover, not integrated into the ancient fabric of the city—a fabric often absent or already destroyed by the voraciousness of urban speculative building—but in the relatively deserted realms of the new settlements, along the highways at certain intersections. For this seems to be the basic characteristic of the shopping mall, to be accessible by car, offering itself as a kind of extra-territorial gift, relaxing and magical to the car-traveller, protagonist and victim at the same time of a fragmented and mobile society.

At the same time, precisely because they ere everywhere, they are nowhere. They are omni-present and unfindable. There is everything inside. The stores have no doors, they open to the outside. Indeed, there is no more idea of an outside and inside. One looks at the merchandise, buys thoughtlessly. The kids can play and run without danger; young and old mix indifferently; the boundaries of age like the parameters of time and place are abolished, cancelled, or, perhaps more precisely, suspended. In fact, the shopping mall is a magic space, a kind of universal Disneyland. It is the kingdom of the big supermarkets, the big chain stores reproduced, careless of environment, with the same features, infinitely, in every location, on the basis of a single determinant: the urge to buy, consume so as to produce once more so as to buy, consume. The sphere of production prevails, and seems at all events divorced from that of consumption. On the other hand, the latter is wholly cut off from real needs. Consumption must be invented, it becomes forced, induced. The market is not sought but created.

For this reason, the shopping mall needs two great institutions of the civilization of the image: television and the highway. Like conversation, face-to-face dialogue between people has been drastically reduced by mass television, so that the little personal store of the street corner has been replaced by the supermarket, replicated in a virtually infinite number of examples on the whole available area. The cocacolization of the world. The shopping mall is its sacred precinct, but it is an open precinct, with no dividing fences, in which all are at the same time celebrants and the simple faithful, free from daily rational duties, "feasting." The hierarchies have fallen, the social classes seem dissolved; age groups are uncertain. This situation has been emphasized with great precision:

The "highway comfort culture" is found everywhere, but does not coincide with any particular location. It is not the city nor yet the suburb or rural America, though it borrows themes and images from these places and transforms them into its own characteristics; it is only . . . *there*, somewhere but nowhere in particular.[1]

History has lost its specific, unique connotations; the social classes are washed away in the indistinct, generalized life style. These are the essential preconditions for the passage from the people to the mass, from a human aggregate still made up of different groups, primary or secondary, face-to-face or bureaucratically organized, to a human powder, spreading out horizontally, shapeless, which is no longer specifically reactive and precisely identifiable. In this process of massification, television plays an important part. The highway changes the physical landscape, joins together the metropolitan centers by excluding from the network the typical villages, the living flesh of the social, the "inside." Television heavily influences psychological makeup. Its development since World War II has been very rapid. Between 1945 and 1950, the number of TV sets went from a few thousand to 15.5 million. The same rate of increase can be found in Italy and other countries, though with an average delay of ten years.

It is also striking that with mass television there should have begun a characteristic process of de-realization. What appears in the shopping mall as a magic moment outside any definite time or place tends with television to become a collective experience. The phenomenon has been partly noted and duly recorded:

Television tends to promote the sale of real merchandise, but does not itself produce real goods. . . . In our market society, the commodity increasingly emphasizes its exchange value so as to make a possible use value useless. If I buy a book and do not read it, that has no excessive importance. If I buy a toothpaste and throw it away without using it, this has no importance for the producer. The only danger lies in the fact that I might not buy any more. This is the threshold beneath which the use value of a product cannot fall; if unusable products are not produced, it is only because their market would collapse. Commercial television is the sole form of commodity in the cultural industry, which in reality realizes its value in being consumed.[2]

However, to achieve this objective it must first seduce its public: that is, place itself alongside the lowest common denominator, understandable to all, accessible to all, and must thus equalize, round off, flatten. At the end of this process the television audience has ceased to be a reactive human whole and has been massified. This does not mean that it has been reduced to the level of troglodytes, vulgar, indecent. On the contrary, massification relates to an average level, neither too high nor too low, in harmony with what the network managers believe to be "conventional wisdom," firmly linked to the values of the "current morality," not as Chesterton feared "run-away morality" but simple, un-problematic morality, ever certain of being right, in black and white. Word and image find in it the highest points of the tension which divides them.

The television screen is an artificial limb, Marshall McLuhan argued. Perhaps. But it is an artificial limb which costs a lot. Television has deprived us already of participation by the human in the human. Conversation is dying. With this the tiniest stories of the everyday are dying out. With the exception of sight, we are probably losing our senses through simple atrophy. Moreover, we do not even have history any more, the history of great events, the story supposed to be connected and explained by the causal nexus. Monocausal explanation must give way to the indeterminate contingency of multifactor analysis. It remains as the desperate, already obsolete, attempt at a dream of logical domination as difficult as it is useless. We are thus painfully torn between two deficiencies. We seek certainties and meet with a void that becomes a shadow. This process has taken place so rapidly that the life of a not particularly long-living man is sufficient to bear witness to another time to more human conditions.

THE PARADOX OF ORAL HISTORY

In the animal warmth of the stables long ago, in a world without telephones, televisions, newspapers, and cinemas, in the long winter nights of my country childhood, stories flourished, old legends bloomed, whilst every day the "social broth" of gossip—that background noise or bass accompaniment of community life—was renewed. A passing gypsy or *pulòt* in the dialect of the lower Vercelli district was at times the source of new, unheard stories. My father had the custom of hosting all the gypsies, the nomads, the *battùsu* and *liggére* who came to our parts. In their bundles, even their rags, the children read the fascination of adventure. In the morning, they had disappeared. They normally paid in advance with the stories told the previous evening. Less exotic and all the more available were the stories of my great-grandmothers Orsola and Battista. These told of French soldiers drowned in the *cavìt* or little channel outside Robelle, the "Rubella" of Fra Dolcino, or the great unexpected holocaust of birds due to a memorable whirlwind towards the middle of the last century. Great history and minimal history, political and military affairs and climatic peculiarities were mixed together and fired the imagination of the audience. For this was the rule: narrators and listeners spoke face to face. The two poles were not separated by the technical apparatus, and they could indeed exchange roles. This is moreover the characteristic of oral history, which makes it the point of intersection, if not the conscious mediation, between the historical story and everyday experience. Between storytellers and listeners the relation is direct, unforeseeable, and problematic. In other words, it is a truly human relation, a dramatic one, without foreseen results. Not only words but gestures, facial expressions, hand movements, even glances, spoke. A direct relation, with immediate feedback, personal reactions, dialogue as a polyphonic moment in which no one present was excluded, as whoever was silent entered the general economy of the collective discourse: his silence permitted the others to speak. This is the gift of the oral: presences, sweat, faces, tone of voice, the meaning—the sound—of silence. The paradox of oral history can be guessed. To be preserved and communicated, or just to be known, oral history has to be written.

Whole phases of the medieval epoch escape investigation because written documents are lacking. While taking due note of the essential difference between written and oral history, one cannot rightly speak of the logical prevalence of writing, the Cartesian separation and distinction between lines, and thus the spatial and mechanically adjunct nature, rather than that of globalizing unity, in the dominant modes of thought up to the invention of printing and publishing. This means, in fact, that writing also entered the open market, with the consequent subordination to the laws of the utilitarian exchange relationship, that is, the acceptance of a certain commercialization of culture and communication flow. It has been observed that medieval scholars can scarcely avoid examining the complex relation between civilization and writing. From the start, with Marshall McLuhan, to W. Ong and Jack Goody, from the paraliterary standpoints to the exegetic and ethnological ones, one point emerges very clearly: the history of *mentalités* and the evolution of modes of thought are linked to the evolution and types of modes and means of communication. The distinctions between sounds are essentially internal. The break comes when, beyond the scribe and copyist, there arrives on the scene the printer. The manuscript still is part of the world of orality.

In this context, Zumthor's observations seem illuminating:

To print (as we are, fortunately, forced to do) a medieval text involves an historical reversal which editorial caution does not manage completely to correct. A test may be the notion of the "authentic text," still today very much alive despite its being periodically questioned—a notion, moreover, of theological origin, paradoxically related to the tradition of the *Word* of God. Whenever a quantity of manuscripts allows us to check their substance, the reproduction of the text basically appears as a re-writing, a re-organization, a compilation. How can we measure the effect of the lapse of time between the production of the text and the first transcription of it? Rather than to a typographic tradition, the vicissitudes of this history resemble those of an oral tradition, and pose problems of interpretation very little different.[3]

However, for a text which is both orality and writing, outside the Eurocentric cultural tradition—a true "founding text"—we may cite the *Geste hilalienne* the account of one of the last bards: an illiterate shepherd of Southern Tunisia tells of a series of epic migrations of the Hilali tribe from the Najd in Saudi Arabia, coming to populate the Maghreb, finishing in Andalusia. Here the oral tradition becomes a collective memory and foundation of the identity of a people; it appears at once as a social phenomenon in action and the institutionalizing of a knowledge, legitimation of tradition, and historical consciousness.[4]

In this sense, oral history is not necessarily the "voice of the past" or at least the voice of a world that is disappearing.[5] It is also the guarantee, the prophecy of a new world which is with difficulty coming to light, or the term of reference of a world which is not resigned to death. Moreover, it is possible to conceive of a use of oral history alternative to that of official historiography. Thus not only is oral history not necessarily and exclusively retrospective, but as instrument for collecting oral testimony, it also appears as a specific means of the everyday listening to itself, a privileged method of critique and demystification of macro-history,[6] as well as an essential integrating moment of it: such as to destroy the artificial counterposing of macro and micro, structure and person. It is not by chance that oral history, in the countries where it is most developed, becomes a valuable instrument for constructing an historical memory of the collectivity above and against the censoring, mutilation, and discrimination of officialdom and traditional historiography. It is not, as is said in a vaguely populistic-sounding way, simplistically "history from below." It is the reconstruction of historical experience in its various, dialectical wholeness. It is the most direct manner of giving the floor to those groups, social classes, and individuals who were traditionally forced into silence or seemed dumb even when they shouted aloud, given that the dominant groups had plugs in their ears and that court historians in their service ruled they did not exist. With oral history even the crowds of illiterates, emarginated, and excluded begin to count. Even if Jules Michelet is considered a typically romantic historian, this is not even romanticism. Rather, it is an enlargement of perspective as regards the history of great men and events and as regards history as a classically academic science.

Where, as in the United States, the "monopoly of the written" seems weaker, oral history develops vigorously. It is true that no one would recount his existential experiences, his *Erlebnisse*, to a tape recorder, but the familiarity and spread of instruments like the recorder, and audio-visual means in general, in this case certainly help. North American oral archives aim at a mass collection of biographies of key personages, mostly belonging to the ruling groups in politics and the economy, transcribed on the basis of relatively standardizable key concepts. The Polish output, especially with the pursuit of Thomas and Znaniecki's studies by J. Chalasinski, has decisively marked that country's sociology, which can count on an extraordinarily rich storehouse of autobiographies. However, aside from the Scandinavian countries, it is perhaps in England that the taste for folklore studies, linked with the traditional collaboration between ethnology and history, has given the most impressive results. In Germany oral history is "alternative history," especially for an unbiased rereading of the Nazi experience. In Italy it becomes the history of those without history, or of the subordinate urban, and even more of the rural, classes.[7] In Joutard's judgment, the situation in France is different. As has been rightly noted, oral history appeared in France in the 1970s, relatively late as regards other European cultures, but precisely for this with an obvious tendency to question itself, to discuss the validity of its own procedures, to reflect critically on its own sources. The possible limits of oral history were especially stressed, as it often seems weak in the face of the temptation to make the past live again without explaining it, accepting it *en bloc* in all its given allusiveness, refusing to criticize the documentation, underrating the theoretical as opposed to the actual, and keeping silent about indispensable conceptual structures. However, it would be difficult to make the relative success of oral history in the most diverse cultural situations simply depend on a breath of populist demagogy. Industrialized societies unexpectedly became aware of the need to glance back, to discover their roots. There is no doubt that the belief in Progress as a kind of lay religion, so self-assured as to transform it into a chronological inevitability, which marked the end of the last century, now appears today, on the threshold of the year 2000, plainly inverted: it has become fear, mistrust, and terror. It is not only a question wich concerns the recent libertarian movements, born of the rebellions and riots of 1968. Even if to many young people today it seems that history really began that year, it is clear that the problem is much older. The myth of inevitable progress[8] has collapsed also through the internal contradictions that gradually drained it, by making the ideal society aimed at coincide with the modern mass, flattened-out societies.

TALKING AMONG HUMAN BEINGS

Behind the success of oral history, which is moreover far from general, given the position of hegemony that specialists in quantitative methods still hold, it is legitimate to discern important psychological variables which concern together with "roots" and the "past," and together with the revival of interest in the sacred and the rural, the process of differentiation and identity. However, one must guard against the risk of psychologizing interpretations. Joutard, for instance, perceives in the fashion for oral history a special, disturbing form of "concern about death." In the very techniques of research in oral history, the way the interview proceeds, he perceives a meaningful link with the idea of death and allows himself an incautious generalization: the interviewee, generally of advanced age, is aware death is approaching; he manages to accept it with serenity, in Joutard's view (even if Freud never tired of saying that when thinking of death we think always of that of other people), only because he can transmit orally his information which otherwise is destined to be lost forever in the grey anonymity of the great "silent majorities."

According to Joutard, it should then be the young interviewer who is disturbed. The story of the interviewee cannot fail to remind him of his own death, a thought he would find less calming and in all likelihood to which he would be resigned less easily than his interlocutor. It is *prima facie* obvious how intellectualist this conception of the dynamics of the interview is, aside from the weakness of the initial hypothesis, which postulates an old interviewee and a young interviewer, taking for granted a generational antagonism that should be tested anyway case by case. It is no wonder that at the end of his analysis Joutard should see in oral history an exorcism of Western culture against death, or, in a positive perspective which is not without plausibility, the new "cult of the dead" of technically advanced industrial societies.

Psychologistic interpretations aside, if we wish to remain within methodology in the broad sense, leaving to one side what we mentioned earlier—the general political meaning of oral history—one can draw useful observations from the scientific premises that make possible the research strategy based on oral history. In fact, this involves a multidisciplinary approach, or, better, postdisciplinary. Disciplines that traditionally ignored each other, such as ethnology, history, sociology, and economics, have finally discovered basic common interests and have managed to define a "new object" for their common scientific research: "mentality," the "collective sensibility." The common person, any man or woman, in other words, everyday life in its specific immediacy, together with the way in which it is recovered, "restored" by the memory which ceaselessly "works" on it, becomes an object of study, examined in an interdisciplinary but unitary manner.

It is here, probably, that one should look for the otherness, the irreducible differentness of oral history, not so much in an explicit political and ideological impulse whereby one tends to favor symmetrically the subordinate over the ruling classes, as rather by bringing into being and developing a history of non-officialdom. This involves everyone, penetrating and breaking down the formal facades, and cuts across institutions, groups, and classes to arrive at the level common to all, apparently microsociological, of the everydayness whereby all human beings are human beings. In this sense, oral history is not necessarily either truer nor more authentic than the official one, even if one can obtain much information only through its accounts, since even oral history, being based on memory, a faculty well known for forgetfulness and in any case highly selective, has its "errors," its commonplaces and mystifing prejudices. Moreover, it is precisely in the slips, the involuntary statements, the silences, and the contradictions as obvious as they are repeated, that the value of its cognitive thrust lies. For it is precisely these cracks or leaks which allow us to reconstruct the "mental representations" which social groups and individuals elaborate in their complex interrelational dynamics. Anyone who has carried out field research collecting life histories and documents of oral history knows there is not only an "official" history of the victors, but also one of the vanquished. There are, and circulate, official versions of the facts and experiences within the counterpowers and extrainstitutional movements, no matter how elastic, spontaneous, and libertarian their manner of being and appearing may be.

What seems fundamental to oral history is the interaction between interviewer and interviewee, an essential characteristic to which we shall turn later, but for the moment it allows us to understand the latent function of oral history as rediscovery of the direct contact, resistance to the process of massification, a rejection (not necessarily crowned with success) of the logic of the mass media and the internal colonization that mass media promote. In current conditions of social communication, the direct interpersonal relation is weakened, is becoming lost. There is nothing conspiratorial in reporting this tendency. It is a statement. It is a statement of a process which appears and presents itself as the result of impersonal forces, neutral, controlled by no one in their specificity. It just happens. Hence we are all to some extent responsible. But when all are responsible, no one is.

To speak of oneself among human beings, not with stereotyped formulas but in depth, calmly, to form and inform oneself at the same time, seems now an increasingly rare luxury. As new specialists emerge, the technicians of the paid confession, so crowds and loneliness paradoxically increase. Certainly, one participates as before: indeed, more than before. But the participation is internally drained, made meaningless, inoffensive. As we are informed, we know everything about everything, but we no longer understand anything. It is a purely cerebral information that does not manage to touch the deeper levels of human beings. It only brushes the skin. At best one takes good note of it, but consequences do not follow as it has no weight, no teeth to grip awareness, no energy to compel one to reorient one's life. Information, especially that provided by the mass media that today have its effective monopoly, and above all the television, now wavers between alibi and an anaesthetic. In the last resort, it fulfills a vocation for narcissism, intrinsic and unsurmountable. *The mass media do not mediate.* They restrict themselves to telling about themselves. They are the origin of the sense of unreality and the process of de-realization that mark modern societies in their high points, where there meet and mix a highly rigorous technical rationality and basic absurdity.

A thick blanket of commonplaces bears upon this situation and prevents its exact perception. It is said that television is a "window open on the world." But we are dealing with a window only seemingly open, and in reality mystifying and essentially closed. In the rarified intimacy of his room, taking refuge in his private dwelling with doors barred, settled into the armchair in slippers, the television viewer participates vicariously in the facts of the world the TV offers, mostly conveniently disinfected, if not sweetened. The more grave and horrible the facts of the "outside" world, the more warm the territory of the private becomes, the more intimate and relaxing the room, the softer and more welcoming the armchair. War, earthquakes, violence, and blood: all the pain of the world seems summoned by a higher, benevolent providence to make the spectacle more enjoyable and instructive for the viewer. For, basically, everything is spectacle. Before ironing out the world, TV flattens out itself. It is a machine for mincing and blending data, experience, and facts and then recomposing them, duly chopped up, devitalized and deprived of specific meaning, for a public hungry for amusement, independently of the contents provided by the programs planned by the managers of the communications business. In the present state of affairs, it is not perhaps premature to state that television is the most effective means of self-complacent mass idiotization the so-called civilized nations have available today.

I do not wish thereby to deny the seriousness and even the sensitivity of certain pedagogic efforts provided by some networks. There are examples that are worth citing. Italian state television once entrusted a well-known journalist with the running of a program called "Dossier" in which by the showing of a film with a social subject, that is, concerning some theme socially and politically important such as the death penalty, terrorism, and civil rights in today's industrialized societies, was preceded and followed by a discussion between experts aided and even enriched by questions and contributions from the audience. This is no comment on the intentions of the organizers, but it soon became clear that it was in the very nature of the medium of mass communication tendentially to distort every theme and content, and for purely technical internal reasons to make it material for a spectacle, rather than using serious problems and questions immediately affecting people in the very real reality of everyday life, by transforming it into mere occasions for amusement and evasion. The social problem chosen for transmission was undoubtedly a real one: its television treatment reduced it to pure theater, a problem to some extent gratuitous.

REALITY AS SPECTACLE

The making of reality into spectacle seems thus to appear as an essential characteristic of the mass media. One should not be scandalized by this. However, the phenomenon, if it is not to be tolerated, must be critically analysed. Television is the real protagonist of this widespread, pervasive holiday spectacular. It is known on the other hand that television, in contrast with cinema, at least for the present, lives on information. The TV eye finds there, in informing, its social function and basic justification. But is it really a matter of information? It has been observed that the problem of information is transformed through television into a "production." It is not by chance that TV attains its peak of truthfulness and "objectivity" when, in an emergency situation, it goes to the spot and records the events with a minimum of technical apparatus and without the assistance of a refined direction. Commonly, instead, in TV transmission, experience seems to be summed up and exhausted in a manner of seeing. Everything seems to exist to be transformed into images. History itself is transformed into a serial, everything played out in two apparently opposing models, in reality converging: uninterrupted banality and inconceivable terror. Thus TV ends up paradoxically transforming reality into a seemingly realistic spectacle. Reality lessens, but in its place there does not arise even the true spectacle of pure representation. There remains only the pseudospectacle of a reality reduced to a specter, a shadow, a caricature of itself.

We have thus reached a phase where even the penetrating observations of Marshall McLuhan are no longer much help. The audio-visual implies a temporal relation with the user which is highly conditioned: the spectator cannot move autonomously in time and is thus basically the passive nursling of an instrument that organizes the layout of his temporal existence. It is not a problem of length, of hours spent in front of the TV or cinema screen. It is a problem of relations and life conditioning. If, after McLuhan, we may say the viewer becomes in turn a screen, we must also admit that the life of this screen is temporally directed and controlled from without, minute by minute. But if the TV transforms reality into a realistic spectacle, then there takes place a transition that I believe to be historically important, from what, for cinema, was an imaginary collective to what, for TV and audio-visuals, can be defined as a collective memory: an accumulation of data and news, which co-exists with our everyday life, also

partly determining it. The boundaries between memory and
the imaginary are very more vague. The imaginary imposes
itself on memory. The world breaks up into images and the
images are the world. The arrival of electronics involves a
series of discourses whose chaotic fascination tends to resemble that of reality, by favoring the illusion of a direct, global,
spatially powerful relation with the world and those who live
in it. A new logic is born, opposed to the traditional, intentional one of mass communications. The logic of the text, of
the communications project, the logic of the point of view (a
McLuhanesque argument). Today there is born the logic of
the double that infinitely repeats itself, the event with the
presumption of making itself instant history, and that must
be immediately memorized, immediately preserved.[9]

It is probable that McLuhan's conception of TV as human
prosthesis is now essentially deficient, but the strong points
of his observation should not be passed over in silence. The
first consists in having disconnected the problem of the mass
media from the question of their effects and good or bad use,
freeing the whole argument from the old moralism which traditionally obscured it. McLuhan had the merit of turning the
problem upside down and telling us these questions were irrelevant as the use was intrinsic to the means. Before this
discovery he tended to express himself in paradoxes, insisting
on the qualitative difference between cinema and television.
The first was projected on the screen and the light came from
behind the spectators, whilst for the second, on the other hand,
the screen is ourselves, the light draws objects on our skin,
and perhaps for this the television tends to condition us
strongly, to tire us, make us its slaves. McLuhan can thus
logically allow us the luxury of casting aside concerns about
video dependency, seeing that TV, through the "message,"
performs a continuous "massage" on the viewer forced to collaborate in the composition of the image. An unforeseen con-
sequence for McLuhan in this interpretation, whether or not
it is technically accurate, is that it is better not to exaggerate
with television. The case of Vermicino, where the TV followed
day and night the desperate, ultimately vain attempt to save
a child who had fallen down a well in the countryside, must

have taught something. In particular, that to treat television as a videotape means to surrender unconditionally to the coils of a celluloid serpent to the point of suffocation, to play irresponsibly with peoples' nerves. For McLuhan, in conclusion, television not only is not predisposed to passivity, but forces participation. One need only add that it can be a suicidal participation.

A second key point of McLuhan's teaching was made clear to me by the attitude of many European intellectuals. They are convinced that McLuhan basically meant that a long season of Western European thought was ending, was dying out. Here there is put on trial the historicist idea that the great intellectuals are the guardians of the temple, the great licensed interpreters of the text, the custodians of the "law." By way of example, one may cite the Frankfurt School and a whole hyperintellectualised critical tradition that saw in ordinary men and women the "mass of damnation" (in St. Augustine's formula). These intellectuals are terrified by manual contamination linked to technical discourse and familiarity with machines. They do not seem able to understand what is happening on the world scale: that the concept of culture—understood as a normative and exclusive one, Eurocentric and prevalently paleo-humanistic in its acceptance of the "beautiful" and the "good" and the Ciceronian *vir bonus dicendi peritus*, legal heir of the Greek *paideia* and Humboldt's *Bildung*—now signifies an attitude that does not manage to understand the others, those different from the classic mold. This attitude denies the man of culture only as the Plutarchian individual, solitary and above the mass of common mortals, who are conceivable as men only in the crudely zoological sense. The historicist tradition linked to this concept of culture is based on the diachronic concept of historical development, on the basis of a unilinear logic which sees in history the realization, step by step and stage by stage, of an idea of man and ideal of life whose guardians, interpreters, and forerunners are the intellectuals as new high priests, sentinels, and watchmen at the same time over "noble values." This elitist, historicist conception is drained from within by McLuhan. Herein lies the explosive character of his contribution. He does not set ideology against ideology, one intellectual construct against another. He does not presume to make ideas give birth to others through parthenogenesis. He confines himself to stating the importance of specific *technical* facts. But the weight of this is amazing.

McLuhan then accuses the paleo-humanist, Eurocentric intellectuals of having become obsolete. His is a kind of open letter to the European intellectuals who have understood human development as if it were only a history of the summit, made up of battles, dynastic marriages, treaties and so on, and not as historical life in the full sense and in its manifold aspects. It seems to me that in McLuhan emerges the first unconscious elements of a new historicity. The unilinear logic of diachronic development diminishes and a new logic advances: that of a co-presence, of the synchronic moment. In a world now forced to be unitarily involved, though at different levels and different ways, perhaps McLuhan is among the first to intuit what this means. A synchronic simultaneity is replacing the diachronic model of unilinear logic that justifies line by line, thereby the variables can be viewed as an interacting whole. We can no longer entrust ourselves exclusively, nor mainly, to visual perception: we must appeal to touch, smell, music, the sense of being together, what he at times called neo-tribalism. It is plain that a whole tradition, also of pedagogy, flooded with intellectualism, is here criticized basically in its preferred schematism. It is not, for example, true that a child today first learns to read, then looks at television. The reverse is true: television comes before the alphabet. Diachronic culture falls and with it the related forms of power. According to certain French intellectuals, the revolution for Algerian independence was not possible because the Algerians were illiterate. Those intellectuals had forgotten one small detail: transistor radios through which the leaders of the resistance gave information, instructions, and orders. The same Eurocentric boast appears today regarding the struggle for the liberation of Palestine, and for the organization of a Palestinian state. There is a desire to legislate an inferiority in principle of the Palestinians in the face of the secret weapon with which their adversaries are supposed to be generously supplied, that is, intelligence. However, aside from the fact that intelligence is not the monopoly of one ethnic group, it is hard to avoid the impression that the Eurocentric boast here is tinged with racism. What McLuhan's intuitions let us understand is, on the other hand, important. Certain forms of retribalization, as it were, and certain "spontaneous" behavior, hinging on the group, especially fashionable among today's youth, are not necessarily to be regarded as a regressive and involuted phenomenon. They may also be presented as the premises for a retaking of the human senses in their wholeness. They can also make it understood how erroneous it is to speak of high and low culture, as every human group is inevitably producer of meanings, signs, and symbols, and hence of culture.

This is an extraordinary point, a truly seminal discovery, opening on to the future. For example, it made me understand, in my studies on the young, the new meaning of music. For me, in the splendid days of my adolescence and first youth, music meant silence, deference, the decorum of Sunday afternoons, mirrors, columns, dinner jackets: the religious-lay atmosphere of the conservatory. The music of today's youth has desacralized this external function of social rite of music. The young live in it: they hear it, they do not listen to it. This has made the return to the classics, from Bach to Mozart, from Vivaldi to Beethoven, on the part of the young a vital experience after the class use the bourgeoisie had made of it. At the same time, McLuhan castigated the arrogance of the pure intellectuals, revealing the sterility of book-worship and proclaiming a type of post-narcissistic culture, which is transformed from *bel canto* to a means of coexistence.

THE AUTONOMY OF THE MEDIUM

It is scarcely necessary to observe that McLuhan also has the vices of some of his undoubted virtues. Perhaps he yields too often to the taste of provocative contamination by mixing technical datum and literary result. This taste for quoting both Shakespeare and optic fibers certainly has an effect of intellectual exhilaration, but by itself it does not prevent miscellaneous gratuitousness and extempore confusions of worlds of thought that are conceptually defined and distinct in themselves, and that cannot be mixed at will without creating general insignificance. To pass in the same paragraph from Plato to St. Thomas Aquinas to Poe provides the refined pleasure of one on the intellectual high-wire: it is certainly a virtuoso exercise. Damage to orderly, logical reasoning may follow, and it often involves the sacrifice of precision to suggestiveness. In McLuhan it is a kind of nervous tic, a drug he cannot give up. Then there is a technological determinism, which seems to approach that of the great realists from Aquinas to Marx, but which rather shows itself as an indifference to the contents of the communication, probably caused by the awareness that in the means of communication there is already a conditioning factor of the communication itself. It is an indifference that, against his own premises, runs the risk of acknowledging an intrinsically pedagogic-formative or de-formative function in the mass media. These functions, however, do not in themselves establish a hierarchic order of knowledges, and thus we find in them the deathly confusion between social communication—as collective, interpersonal communication—and intentional communication, directed by an end which allows and indeed compels the reordering of the empirical data. This problem, however, does not detract much from his discovery of the relative autonomy of the medium regarding the meaningfulness of the transmission, a discovery that moreover suffers from two absences: time and historical knowledge. However, one who has, like him, a synchronic vision of phenomena is also a prophet. He sees everything on the same level, the fall of Jerusalem and the end of the world. McLuhan was without the sense of time, just as the political instinct was weak or atrophied in him.

Yet it is hard and perhaps improper to speak of McLuhan without returning to his ignored master, Harold Adams Innis. Though McLuhan rapidly became an internationally known figure in the field of communications research and its instruments, Innis is still today relatively unknown. The paradoxical aspect of the situation, which would justify a specific study of the sociology of cultural processes by itself, is that Innis was to all effects the master and inspiration of McLuhan. That was naturally acknowledged by McLuhan himself with a candor and admiration which in reality are rather rare. "I have the impression when thinking of my book *The Gutenberg Galaxy* [U. of Toronto Press 1962] of a footnote to Innis's remarks on the psychological and social consequences first of writing and then of printing" (from the introduction to Harold A. Innis, *The Bias of Communication*, University of Toronto Press, 1951, p. ix). This is not a formal acknowledgment. McLuhan explains in what way the "tendentiousness" of the communication brought out by Innis's studies helps us to set up and correctly carry out research on cultural processes. It comes, even though at first sight it does not seem clear, from his research on the fur trade and other aspects of economic life, with special reference to tendentially subordinate economic systems with regard to both economic and cultural structures in a clearly hegemonic position.

Think, in this regard, of the situation of the Canadian economy with respect to the American. But one must not thus fall into the easy interpretative trap of enclosing Innis into the framework of a fashionable Marxism. Rather, we are in the presence of a historically very aware attitude, sensitive to the dynamic interrelations and the basic interconnections of social experience, which clearly recalls both Thorstein Veblen and Arnold Toynbee, as McLuhan duly remarks. In this sense, the Italian translation of this basic work by Amelto Lorenzini (*Le tendenze della comunicazione*, Sugarco, Milan, 1982) though valuable, by rendering the term "bias" as "tendencies" rather than "tendentiousness," runs the risk of losing sight of the meaning and theoretical premises of Innis's research.

This research is basically concerned with the problem of power as a total social phenomenon. Thence derives its modernity and lasting value. McLuhan understood this very well.

Most writers provide summaries of the contents of philosophy, science, libraries, empires and religions. Innis instead invites us to consider the modalities of power exercised by this structure through their reciprocal interaction. Innis approaches each of these forms of *organised power* as though it exercised a particular kind of force on each of the components. All the components exist by virtue of processes which alternate between both, and all. (Quoted from the translation by A. Lorenzini, p. 13, emphasis in original.)

The presentation of Innis's thought by McLuhan is extraordinarily incisive. What is surprising is that McLuhan himself had not made use of all the positive potential already present in Innis's outlook. Innis's attention to the technical factor is reduced in McLuhan to a crude technological determinism, often dangerously vitiated by mechanism, hasty and unilateral. In other words, while in Innis there is a lively sense of dialectical globality and the interconnectedness of the social, McLuhan apparently did not understand that the mass media do not mediate and thus tend to lead us into the deadly confusion between *social* communication as collective communication, and *intentional* communication directed by an end and maintained by a criterion of priorities that allow the reordering of the empirical data and close off the danger of being swallowed up. Finally, McLuhan, as given by his sociobiological orientation lacks *time*, with the related problem of cumulative succession, the historical dimension, and integration. But it is really to the problem of time that Innis is very sensitive. He remains a historian, open to the search for material relations of life and the study of the modes of interaction between the various structures that together make up the social.

Long before the recent studies by Fernand Braudel and Jacques Le Goff, Innis distinguishes the various conceptions of time according to different societies and within each according to different social classes and professions. Some passages from the essay "In Defence of Time" deserve quotation:

In Western civilization a stable society depends on a just balance between the concepts of space and time: the characteristic of the medium of communication is that of creating a prejudicial tendency in the civilization, intended to favor the concept of time, or that of space (Le tendenze della comunicazione, p. 86).

The examples Innis offered bear witness to an erudition and cultural breadth which are quite remarkable:

In the agricultural system dependent on irrigation, the measurement of time becomes important for predicting the periods of flooding, the important dates of the year, the time of sowing and harvesting. Interest in time was a reflection of the importance of religion and the choice of the periods in which festivities could be celebrated (p. 87).

Moreover,

The Babylonian clergy with their interest in time contributed to the study of astronomy and astrology with the introduction of the chronological system in the era of Nabonassar in 747 B.C. . . . The limited possibility of political organizations expanding their control over space to counterbalance the clergy, who held the monopoly of knowledge of time, facilitated the development of marginal organisations like that of the Jews in Palestine (*op. cit.*, p. 89).

On the other hand,

There followed on the restriction of writing in relation to the sacred book and the limitations of legal and ritual manner in the Koran the growth of the oral tradition with the Hadith, a new saga which replaced the old prose of sage of the Arabs (p. 141).

What is crucial in Innis's thought is precisely the control of time and space, especially the monopoly positions. There is no neutral communication. Nor is it a matter of showing, as McLuhan did later, that every message is already in itself a message, and thus the medium is the content. For Innis, the publication of the writings on communication and empire (cf. H. A. Innis, *Empire and communication*) and earlier in the studies of the fur trade, it is clear that every means of communication is determined in view of control of time or space. His specific and original contribution lay in the systematic exploration of the types and modes of control internal to means of communication. In his view, the rise and fall of empires is explained by examining the types of monopolies of time and space, conceived of as two inversely proportional variables. Societies enter a state of crisis and endemic instability with the upsetting of the balance between time and space. For this reason, every form of monopoly that stressed the prevalence of control of time or space presented itself as a danger to society, in that it blocked the dynamic of development and the competitive conflict between the various social structures. (See on this the essays of James W. Carey, especially "Harold Adams Innis and Marshall McLuhan," and "The Mythos of Electronic Revolution," and, with John Quirk, "Canadian Communication Theory: Extensions and Interpretations of Harold Innis.")

THE CONTRIBUTION OF HAROLD ADAMS INNIS

It may give rise to surprise to have to remark that here McLuhan is a clear step back in relation to Innis's analysis. His work is certainly less compressed and more brilliant. But these gifts, which only the biased could contemptuously cast aside as deplorable examples of "cogitus interruptus," are also the necessary premise for an out-datedly psychologizing conception of social relations. The risk, moreover, concerns all the theoretical aspects of the communication in which who communicates and who is communicated with does not emerge sufficiently clearly; but it is a risk from which Innis seems reasonably distant, and which to all appearances does not threaten his work. Since the splendid conference on *The Press— A Neglected Factor in the Economic History of the Twentieth Century* Innis never lost sight of the basic elements of individual psychological attitudes. For example,

The implications of the twentieth century press are indicated by the growing importance of evening newspapers as against morning ones. Evening papers go to individuals who have exhausted their possibilities of concentrated mental effort and need amusement and relaxation rather than information and instruction (p. 48).

From this Innis drew stimulating observations on the extraordinary possibilities for manipulation for elements of the printed page, aided if not speeded up by the invention of a new language and its victory over the traditional one, especially where it did not run up against the barrier of a well-backed and socially respectable classical culture. Here are clear points of contact with, on one hand, the thought and analyses of Thorstein Veblen and on the other with structural Marxist analyses, but also with the critique of technology developed by, among others, Oswald Spengler and Ortega y Gasset, which official Marxism wrongly obliterated too summarily on the basis of a purely dogmatic outlook. Beyond and in some ways against his pupil McLuhan, Innis's lesson should be taken up again in all its significance.

Innis must be understood in his specific context. He was a Canadian citizen: he thought and wrote on the basis of the demands of his environment and the needs of his culture. He believed that no sociological research at the critical level could be developed in a historical void, in a "pure" state, without the weight of a precise "ethnocentric tendentiousness."[10] He never tired of polemics against the claim of universality by the American social sciences, so ingenuously sure of working out a universally valid argument, of fixing—as Talcott Parsons, among others, thought he had managed—the "evolutionary universals" of all industrializing societies. This pushed them to theorize the social system as a given; American society in its current historical specificity, and at the same time as ideal normative term, by whose yardstick all other societies on a world scale should be evaluated to determine their level of civic maturity and technical efficiency. For Innis, being a Canadian citizen meant finding oneself in a paradoxically privileged situation, belonging to a culture and country cheek by cheek with the American giant, having in common its language and a series of economic interests, and at the same time having to keep one's distance and assert one's own identity so as not to be totally absorbed and risk being culturally swallowed up and historically annihilated.

Thus for Innis it was not a matter of silly nationalistic pride, but rather of national survival and autonomy. He was aware that one must resist the hegemonic pressure, intellectual but also economic and political, of the United States, not only for the defense of the Canadian homeland but to prevent the assertion of a social science without any explanatory value, tending to project its own schemas and preconstituted conceptual categories on a reality whose special characteristics had not even been touched on. From this point of view it is hard to exaggerate Innis's importance regarding the power linked to the technical monopoly of the United States with regard to the mass media and their programs. To take a banal but significant example, think of the exportation throughout the world of the TV series "Dallas." In Egypt, to cite a non-European country, TV is wholly taken over by Islamic religious programs: the only exception is the "lay" broadcasting of "Dallas." The same is true for other countries for the soap operas and telenovellas, "stories for TV." What characterizes these programs is the fact that they never finish, they are never-ending. The story from one episode to the next stretches to infinity. It touches on problematic themes and situations with undoubted realism, but at the same time outside any specific historical context, hinging on impulses and elementary behavior (sex, power, money) that concern and involve everyone, but no one in particular. The delight, pleasure, and obvious favor with which similar programs are followed by crowds of viewers belonging to the most various political and cultural traditions are naturally invoked by the producers as an authoritative confirmation of the "goodness" of the product. But other explanations for the exceptional "enjoyment indexes" are possible. One notes an undeniable tendency, increasingly widespread, to take refuge from mental efforts, even those the reading of a book involves. One of the probable factors is the very satiety of receiving daily information through the images of the ever-present domestic screen, replacing the traditional forms of family dialogue. It has been rightly observed that the semihypnotic condition in which most people follow TV broadcasts often leads, apart from a considerable difficulty with and distaste for expressing one's own ideas coherently, to a series of real dyslexic disturbances, especially the inability to distinguish between written words, written fully, and those abbreviated, with a subsequent tendency to write the first part of syllables and difficulty in placing accents. The atrophy of the imagination thus leads progressively to reducing the habit of reading and at the same time the satisfaction induced by the contemplation of images, even better if the words no longer appear, as still happens in the comics.

We are faced with a new form of illiteracy which prefers acquiring knowledge through images. The television public and the mass of avid consumers of audio-visuals can certainly believe themselves technically very advanced, but it is hard not to compare them, in certain important respects, to the processions of the faithful in the Middle Ages, for whom were designed the frescoes in the great basilicas and cathedrals where the lives of the saints were illustrated for edification, beyond any personal, critical parameters. Nor is statistical confirmation lacking. As regards the United States, the numerous remedial reading classes for twenty-year-olds who are practically illiterate are no longer a luxury but a simple necessity. In Italy more than 20,000 books are published every year, of which at least 3,000 are literary works. In the school libraries there are calculated to be about 25 million volumes. Yet as regards the reading of the young, the prospects are pessimistic. Not only the young, but Italians in general, read little. Only 47 percent read at least one book a year. Such a depressed cultural situation has, however, found its ingenious apologists. It has been observed:

Italian society has an ancient tradition of creativity and knowledge through images, since the Renaissance. Renaissance civilisation, in fact, was largely a visual one. Further, as distinct from what has been shown in France and Germany for example, in Italy mass literacy and long schooling arrived when already the media of communication were no longer limited to the book and newspaper. The contact between the Italians and school and reading largely coincided with the arrival of mass circulation periodicals, of specialist weeklies and monthlies "in pictures," of TV and so on. In short, an old visual civilisation mingles with an information system dominated by the broadcasting of images. Hence derives a different system of communication which cannot be schematically compared with that of other countries. It is true we read fewer papers, but all, including the young, read more weeklies: they inform themselves differently, even with television. Thereby the sum of news, all in all, which arrives at the consumer in Italy as elsewhere in Europe is more or less the same. Thus, if as the outset the channels are different, it does not seem that in the end, in the output, the culture and preparedness of Italians are very different from those of other European countries. Newspapers and books, periodicals and monthly reviews like the *Reader's Digest*, informatics and computers, TV and videotapes, radio and "cultural" comics, are a single whole, and shower on us a flood of news: all this makes us more alike than at one time.[11]

This really means sweet talking and putting one's conscience to rest cheaply. And yet language itself is a valuable, pitiless spy. It is not yet certain if the news that floods down on the unfortunate reader of comics or the TV viewer or audio-visual fan helps to inform, to shape or misshape, or to meticulously prepare—but not too much—a generation devoted to passive voyeurism or a people of well-informed idiots, who can discuss everything but without formulating a personal critical judgment on anything. Here a rather delicate matter is touched on, on which Innis has already said something important and which I allow myself to recall, having dealt with it fully elsewhere.[12] The source of the "flood of news" is discretely left in the shadows. The risk of a crude conspiratorial outlook is clear, and this risk has not always been avoided by the generous but ingenuous analyses carried out by the polemical initiatives of counterinformation. But Innis correctly confronts the question:

When Innis spoke of monopolies of knowledge, his examples often concerned physical and structural problems: speed of movement and access to stored information. However, he also used the term in its stronger sense. *He believed that the basic form of social power was the power of defining what reality is.* The monopolies of knowledge in a cultural sense thus refer to the attempts of certain groups to determine the global vision of the world of a people: to produce, in other words, an official view of reality which can constrain and control human action.[13]

KNOWLEDGE AND INFORMATION

The monopoly of knowledge is not even dented when its owners say they are ready to offer anyone requesting them the tapes of their data banks, and to guarantee access to all the information in their possession. It is not a matter of this. The real problem lies in placing under discussion, and thus submitting to a rigorous sceptical questioning, the general conception that lies beneath the production and storing of data through computers and their tapes. In other words, the question concerns the technocratic vision of the world, on the basis of which one decides what is an important fact or meaningful datum, and on which the very concept of truth depends, here reduced to a sequence of disconnected facts, perfectly quantifiable and storable, made manageable and interchangeable under the headings of convenient items. One should not confuse knowledge with an aggregate of information. Any knowledge of reality necessarily refers back to a theoretico-conceptual apparatus which, like an invisible but determining scaffolding, makes the link with the reality of the world at the very moment this is explored and, as it were, systematically ordered. In fact, nothing is given that is immediately observable. The monopoly of knowledge does not so much refer to specific information, more or less fragmentary, but rather to the theoretico-conceptual apparatus underlying it, and its inevitable criteria of selection. In this way it is clear that the monopoly of knowledge is not to be crudely reified like a kind of exclusive right over a certain quota of information. Rather this becomes concrete in the relation between a given form of communication, in its double, intellectual and structural-technical aspect, and the vision of the world this form holds and sustains, and thus makes possible and plausible. From this viewpoint, proposing as key term or basic explanatory criterion of historical evolution the form of communication (in preference to the source of energy or any other determining factor), Innis can distinguish four large phases of transformation of the social organization in the history of the West: the imperial unification of the Upper and Lower Nile, essentially based on writing and mathematics, the availability of papyrus as a light and cheap form of communication, engineering, and the navigation of the Nile; the second, coinciding with the Roman Empire, still based on writing and papyrus, but also road-building and the spread of the horse and *ibiga*;

thirdly, that of the modern European empires, linked to the press, navigation on the high seas, mining, and later steam (what Patrick Geddes called "paleo-technical civilization"; finally, the modern one dominated by the two tendentially ecumenical imperial systems, American and Soviet, essentially linked to the use on an ever-widening scale of electricity and electronics, petroleum and reactors. It is precisely with this last phase that Innis is least concerned. On the other hand, it is hard to deny that his best-known pupil, Marshall McLuhan, far from critically developing Innis's position, rapidly stranded on a kind of triumphal hymn to technology, in the spirit and at times even the letter of a triumphalistic catalogue à la Whitman—a willing victim of the technocratic myth who saw in the simple technical application of electricity and electronics the painless solution to all political and social problems.[14]

Much more refined in comparison, though technically obsolete, is the apology for the mass media set out by Paul F. Lazarsfeld. It is curious how this ex-socialist Viennese, transplanted to the United States, should then have worked with such dedication for the defense of the mass media. To discover the practical cause of the theoretical error, it should be ascribed to the need to protect the Bureau of Applied Social Research founded by him and managed from the institutional setting of Columbia University. But such discoveries are never enough nor are they exhaustive. Lazarsfeld, together with his collaborators, must be confronted in intellectual terms, as it is in these that he presents himself. With his collaborators, he first of all rejects the dichotomous vision that sees on one side the omnipotent means of mass communication and on the other the defenseless, atomized, and thus manipulable at will, individual: an undistinguishable part of a shapeless mass. According to Lazarsfeld, between the "mass" and the "medium" there is the small group, with its whole informal but real network of channels of information, its structure, the web of interpersonal relations not easily explorable scientifically, but determining. The power of the mass media must thus be decisively recalculated. Society on the other hand is not an abstraction. It is made up of individuals with houses, families, neighbors, and colleagues. The messages of the mass media do not pass directly to the individual, do not bombard his living flesh. They must pass through the dense filter of the small informal group and come to terms with its real but elusive influence. Hence, from the theoretical and empirical viewpoint, there comes the need to explore and evaluate the effects of the mass media in connection with the study of the small informal group; hence, further, there comes the hypothesis of a communication flow which has two phases—the two-step flow of communication—and the heuristic need to employ instruments capable of measuring its impact.[15] If indeed the small primary group, within which the concrete everyday life of the individual develops, performs a determining function regarding the acceptance or rejection, or indifference, regarding the messages of the means of mass communication, it is clear that it becomes cricial to establish on the basis of what selection criteria the messages are chosen, in the interest of whom, for what ends, and favoring or censoring what contents. This is not the time to enter into the technical details of Lazarsfeld's research, but it should be remarked that the sole fact of hypothesizing the existence of a critical filter between mass media message and receiver of their action was enough to suspend doubt on the apocalyptic vision of mass society as outlined by a series of critics, variously oriented from a political and ideological point of view, but all unanimously disposed to see in mass society the end of classical humanistic culture, or the only true culture.

Was Lazarsfeld's discovery really a discovery or only the unconscious nostalgia of the Viennese immigrant, the memory of the intimate warmth of an organized, static society, like the Austrian, both echo and romantic memory, jealousy laid and guarded in the deep recesses of the soul, of a lost *Gemeinschaft* of Toenniesian derivation? In other words, is there really a small informal primary group and does it have a real weight in current metropolitan conditions? Have you ever heard someone in Manhattan calling the neighbors from a window as is done in some districts in Naples? Is it not perhaps the very architecture that forbids it? Are what used to be called the "street corner societies" alive and active? Can one really,

not just metaphorically, speak of urban villagers, joining the
two perspectives so subtly set out by Musil in *The Man without Qualities*, or overcoming the divergence between the two
life-styles so eloquently drawn by Georg Simmel? The law of
the market, and the commodification deriving therefrom, have
been imposed and by all accounts are gaining ground on a
world scale. Immediate utility and maximization of profits are
destroying all the margins not directly utilitarian that tradition, custom, hospitality, the simple taste for being together,
had once fed. Lazarsfeld must have forgotten Gabriel Tarde's
essay on *La conversation*, which he too, moreover, cites in his
methodological writing.[16] No, it is useless to live on illusions.
The conversation has been interrupted. The thread of the direct interpersonal tale has been snapped. And it was precisely
the queen of the mass media, the ever-present television, which
broke it, with its great cyclopean eye open day and night, the
brand-new totem watching over the now dumb house where
the dialogue has been extinguished, absorbed and replaced by
its chattering repetitious voraciousness. I have already remarked that we have thus returned to the basic contradiction
that underlies the brilliant individualist-atomistic construct
of Tarde and that at the same time reveals Lazarsfeld's apol-
ogetic intention with regard to the mass media and their social role. The image, the iconic message (even supposing it
has filtered through the small group, which is said to be located between the media and the mass), at the moment it permits the greatest return with minimal expense, really de-
frauds us of real human knowledge and participation, one which
is unpredictable and dramatic. Life touches us, but through
an intermediary. It is a reflected life which does not live, an
intimated life, the shadow of a shadow. It is by definition a
life of rubble. Being a spectator disposes one to passive participation, vicarious enjoyment. It is the antechamber of mental
passivity and political inertia, the necessary premise to a manipulation which, in the case of technically advanced and sufficiently depersonalized and dynamic societies becomes a kind
of internal colonization and proletarianization of the soul: or
a resolution and subsuming of the individual into the schema
production-consumption-production. No one lives any more. One

is impersonally lived. From start to finish the individual is simply weakened, flattened, and homogenized to the point of dissolving.

THE PROLETARIANIZATION OF THE SOUL

It was presumed that the small primary group should have functioned as a critical filter regarding the torrential messages of the mass media. But the small group did not survive. In reality it was culturally emarginated and physically and historically annihilated. The small group no longer exists, the free trade area of the interpersonal. The undifferentiated mass of users exists. Its desert flatness, its shapeless, seemingly docile, jellied softness, as of human jam, has struck the imagination of literary figures and aesthetic analysts:

The mass has no attributes, no subject, no quality, no reference. This is its definition, or rather its radical indefinition. It has no sociological "reality." It has nothing in common with a *real* population, no body, no specific aggregate. Any attempt to qualify it is only the effort to convert it into sociology, and tear it from that indefinition which is not even that of equivalence (the infinite sum of equivalent individuals, $1+1+1+1$, this is the sociological definition), but rather that of the *neutral*, that is *neither the one nor the other* (ne-uter).[17]

Baudrillard too assuredly confuses sociology, which is capable of globalizing critical analyses, with descriptive sociography. To say, as he does, that the mass is the black hole into which the social sinks and disappears is the same as refusing to attempt analysis and an intelligible explanatory discussion. It is true that one must not fall into metaphysicalizing essentialism, like Gustave Le Bon's,[18] but one must also guard against the suggestive phrases that restrict themselves to making metaphors of social phenomena instead of going forward with their analysis. Undoubtedly the mass is essentially distinguished from other basic sociopolitical categories. It is different from the people, the community, the social class. It is certainly a collective aggregate, but until the great conductor, the charismatic chief, touches its secret chords, it remains an unfeeling, amorphous whole, a gelatinous reality waiting for someone to mold it. The means of mass communication are precisely "mass" because they are situated from the viewpoint of the communication flow and chain, at the lowest level, and also for this reason the mass can be at the same time, apparently contradictorily, both crowd and lonely. The mass (the shapeless and passive aggregate) is at the same time suffused with messages of the mass media and tied, that is, variously conditioned on the basis of the impulses, information, and messages received, without being given the specific possibility of a reciprocal action.

But is it really like this? Is there really the mass-man, the neoslave, the docile victim ready to collaborate with his executioner? To what point can the messages of the mass media penetrate and spread without meeting passive resistance—techniques of adaptation, assimilation, and distortion—often unexpected and doubtless provided with a certain originality? In the discussions of the mass it is not hard to perceive an ancient echo of a theological kind, which moreover shines forth from the very nature, absolutizing and dogmatic, of theories about the masses, and their totalizing catastrophism: the age of the masses is presented as the age of a divine curse or great epidemic. The masses have a blind power, but are not for this less capable of deadly infections. The arrival of the masses in the first years of this century is described by Ortega y Gasset as the "revolt of the masses," and one's mind runs to the servile throngs leaving in rebelling groups from the catacombs of history. It is elite culture that feels endangered, as the old families of Rome felt threatened when, after they had lived for centuries in Piazza di Spagna, the subway connecting the famous square with the most outlying suburbs was built. They felt invaded every Sunday evening by barbarian hordes and complained "our peace is finished, our drawing-room ruined."

In this perspective, the mass media are a basic instrument of social subjection, the stick and carrot of the new barbarians. They conduct the uprooting to perfection, and they crudely unveil the conditions of exploitation that make possible the civilization of the happy few, their refined manners, their courtesies, and the little things that make life worth living.

The masses have entered into history, have just appeared in the first person and take their place on the stage, when suddenly there comes into operation the mechanisms of a new, more insidious, and deeper slavery. The potential individual in them dies before being born. After physical exploitation, after the alienation connected to the sale of physical labor-power to the highest bidder on a violently asymmetrical market, there begins the age of vertical exploitation, internal colonization, the draining of nervous energy, the sale of loyalty and personal dignity, the expropriation of individual ability to judge. We are watching the agony of the individual as subject both autonomous and self-sufficient. Perhaps the days are numbered for this Leibnizian monad. The Enlightenment dream of constant, unstoppable progress under the banner of an individualism rationally provided for in the face of nature and society has been turned into its opposite. We live in an age of uncertainty, disintegration, and violence. Such practices as torture, believed to have been forever consigned to the dark ages of history, are revealed as the daily custom of governments held to be "civil."

The subject, the Ego, the I is a relatively recent Western conquest, and all in all a fragile one. For the ancients, man realized himself in the public sphere, in the service of the state. To acknowledge Jacob Burckhardt, the very birth of the individual in Italy, his development in Renaissance civilization, and his formation as source of personal, unpredictable decisions are to be sought in the nature of the states and principalities which made up Italy at that time. Burckhardt remarked:

The nature of these states, be they republican or despotic, was the main if not the only cause of the early development of the Italian. It was above all thanks to that that he became a modern man. It is again thanks to that that he was the first of the children of modern Europe. In the Middle Ages, the two faces of consciousness, the objective and the subjective, were in some way veiled. Intellectual life was like a doze. The veil wrapped round the spirits was woven of faith and prejudices, ignorance and illusions: it made the world and history appear in odd colors. . . . Italy was the first to tear off this veil and gave the signal for the *objective* study of the State and all the things of this world; but alongside this manner of viewing objects there developed the *subjective* aspect: man became a spiritual *individual* and acquired consciousness of this new condition."[19]

THE HUMAN VOICE IN ATHENS

Burckhardt recalls that expressions like the "singular," or the "single" man began to have currency then. They pointed to the "superior men" or even the "universal men," such as Leon Battista Alberti. They were unheard-of expressions of an absolute originality, which marked and attributed a value to the individual in himself, independently of the social or public functions he performed, hence removing him from his position in the community and the State. It was an idea of the individual that was linked to self-awareness, in ways we shall find—developed and perfected—in Montaigne and Rousseau. Now it is true that in the first book of the *Confessions*, Rousseau says he was inspired in his earliest childhood years, and perhaps shaped, by reading aloud, till deep into the night and at times till morning, Plutarch's *Parallel Lives* to his watchmaker father in Geneva. But for Plutarch and the classics in general, individual life had meaning and merited telling about only as public function. In the *Origines*, Cato the Elder boasted of not having mentioned a single proper name. The biographies of the Greeks were *enkomia*, funeral orations, recited for the edification of the citizens in the presence of the corpse. In the classics, man is never defined as such, immanently. He might be defined by exclusion, by differentiating him simultaneously from the gods and the animals. He might be defined on the basis of the position he occupied in society or in view of a divine, heavenly hierarchy, in terms of transcendental ideas grounding him, guaranteeing his soul or noble element, not subject to death, physical decline or the corruption which seems to await bodies as their inevitable end. However, man was never defined as "internal man," as a value in himself. One cannot say that in this respect Christianity produced radical innovations. Christian interiority did not have value in itself: it had value and counted in that it opened the gates of paradise and eternal life. "Non habemus hic manentem civitatem," St. Paul said, with dry clarity, precisely worthy of a professional soldier. On the other hand, the case of St. Augustine and his *Confessions* is extraordinarily instructive. His *edifying* intent reveals his pseudomodernity. This makes him fall outside the coordinates of Western individualism: outside, that is, the conception of the individual as *causa sui*, an an autonomous reality, independent and self-sufficient. Unlike Rousseau or Stendhal, Benvenuto Cellini or Goethe, St. Augustine does not confess to himself. Though his is a closed dialogue and at times a dramatic encounter between the *ego inferior* and the *ego superior*, St. Augustine confesses himself essentially to God, calls God to account, and demands explanations for the inscrutable designs of his destiny. Basically it is God speaking to God in the courthouse of Augustine's conscience. The individual is only a go-between, the occasion and sign of a transcendent presence in the world.

In Rousseau, on the other hand, as moreover in Montaigne, the individual is both end and means. Rousseau's *Confessions*, like Stendhal's *Memoirs of an egoist* (*Souvenirs d'égotime*) are the vivisection of an individual experimenting on a live body, surgery on himself, a descent to the nether regions of an immanent interiority, closed upon itself, too disenchanted to believe or hope in an otherworldly design. Rousseau does not accept himself as he is: mad, ungrateful, multiple and hence faithloɔɔ, porhapɔ ɔchiɔoid. Ho iɛ too much a child of hiɛ timo: an elightened, rationalist individual *malgré lui*. He cannot accept incoherence. He feels and proclaims his faults. He hopes thereby to be absolved. Stendhal, on the thread of memory, departs from today to go back in time. He was not unlike Mark Twain in this, who gave himself up to free association as against all chronological sequence, with a shame, however, which Rousseau and Chateaubriand did not know. It is hard to write an autobiography without writing on oneself, or even without speaking, or speaking with the dry impersonality of the articles of the civil code. Autobiographers are frustrated gossips. Quoting Emmanuel Lévinas, Béatrice Didier remarked that to the extent the autobiographer tries to show his face, he stirs the word. Face and speech are linked. The face speaks. It speaks in that it makes possible and starts off every discussion. It is hard to be silent in someone's presence. This difficulty has its basis in the real meaning of speech, whatever is said. One has to speak of something, the rain or the fine weather, it scarcely matters, but to speak, to reply *to* him and so reply about him. "The reader of autobiographies runs the risk of speaking too much."[20]

However, this idea of the individual, the theme of autobiographies, observing itself with participant distance each day, in its internal movements, its leaps and falling back, the point of departure and of arrival, which has the presumption to sum up in itself human evolution, now appears obsolete; it is no longer homogeneous with technically advanced mass societies and corresponds decreasingly to their functional imperatives. Today, the Ego is in flight. The demands made on him/it fragment him on multiple levels whose non-contradictoriness is by no means assured. Perhaps it is true that the individual is becoming nothing more than the surrounding of the system, the chance crossroads of tensions and trajectories which are superimposed, denied, or are cumulated with supreme indifference. The individual is dissolved in the group and the community, seeks margins—plastic, shifting, and precarious—of survival within the great formal bureaucratic organizations, appears under the lying guise of a weak, de-subjectivized subjectivity, which refuses to present itself as the exclusive depository of "noble values." The normative paradigm of rationality and moral values changes. The problems that face the individual today are no longer an individual fact. Nationality has abandoned him: it has become an essential characteristic of impersonal organizations. The exalting of the subject has an unbearable rhetoric, based on a predatory thought that is unable to understand, as it is unable to listen. The acritical exaltation of the individual is unacceptable today as it is linked to a Eurocentrism which, rhetoric and civilizing mission aside, has been historically specialized and made famous through despotic domination, racial persecution, and mass physical and moral genocide. One should not be surprised that at the end of humanistic individualism and the identity of the subject, as a given, frozen situation, is now a recurring theme. At the existential level too, the dissolving of the subject is an acquired awareness. The place of the subject has long been un-inhabited. It has become the place of the Other. Perhaps we are witnessing the end of "egology."

Along with the end of the subject we are present at the end of that instrument of intellectual fornication and subtle soli-tary pleasures *par excellence*, the book. We are returning to orality. The spoken word appears victorious over the written word and the printed page. No one writes letters any more. One calls. We want the "viva voce" of the friend, the fiancée, one's loved ones, but also of enemies and victims, even of the relatives of those kidnapped. It is a new orality, a group rite, the choral voice of a new tribalization in whose fresh, luke-warm water the lofty, elitist nineteenth-century individual-ity, the *Kulturmensch*, internally secure and oriented, is little by little sinking. The word is gaining the upper hand. The audio-visual media are winning. The ear is beating the eye. But the spoken word, the new orality, must face up to the technical apparatuses that support it and diffuse it with a rare efficiency, but at the same time condition and coopt it, enslave it to the point of transforming it into an appendix or purely instrumental accessory. I ask myself how Demosthenes could speak in Athens in the square without a microphone.

What was the human voice in Athens? When I take the floor in a meeting today, I am taking part in a round table, or I am intervening in a discussion, and my voice does not pass directly from me to my interlocutors but is filtered and ampli-fied by the microphone. This now-indispensible gadget is not without its moods: at times it croaks with bouts of sinister huskiness as though catarrh was about to choke it. At other times it produces along with the voice a thin snakelike hiss, which seems to proclaim mystification if not downright lying. In the collective imagination, moreover, the loudspeaker has now won the position of symbol and instrument of coercive officialdom, the canal through which there pass at a volume and with tones at once stentorian and anonymous, instruc-tions for use by the waiting mass. The oceanic rallies of the totalitarian regimes had their privileged technical means in the loudspeaker, from the surging crowds in Piazza Venezia during the fascist regime in Italy to the nighttime Wagnerian parades in Nuremburg. I am trying, as a natural comparison, to imagine what the human voice was and how it was revealed in the public places of Pericles' Athens. The acoustics of the marketplace must have been so perfect that Demosthenes had no need of the microphone. Nor must the orator have had to use special effort. The voice, well produced, did not require special strain on the vocal chords. It was borne on the sweet lightness of the wind, and speaking in public did not hinder the subtlety of the reasoning, which is normally met with in dialogue between a few people in private. The orator did not need to be a shouter.

However, there is no doubt that the logic of the spoken word, the public discussion, has very little to do with the logic of the written word, printed and published in a considerable number of copies, such as to take on its special autonomy as a printed work. The speaker stands before his interlocutors; one can observe him from nearby. Not only does one listen to what he says, but one can see his sweat, facial expression, the movements of his hands and eyes, all the gestures that accompany, emphasize, and comment on the speech, with its inflections, pauses and rhetorical questioning. Then one should consider the spontaneity, the immediacy, the being unable to go back. The spoken word remains. It cannot be rubbed out. One says: *verba volant: scripta manent.* Really? But it is the spoken word which does not, once it is pronounced, admit repentance. Unlike the written word, it is not permitted to undertake the laborious operation of editing, with its additions, cuts, emphases, and re-touching, up to the final version. This is the great qualitative difference between theater and cinema. Moreover, it has been remarked that the written word, as it appears in the book, obeys a spatial logic based on the separateness of one line from the next, and that this cannot simply be reduced to a technical-typographical fact. It predisposes the reader to fragment and subdivide the thought into its components according to the Cartesian rule which in the frist place demands "clarity and distinction." From this logically analytical position, a return to the global consideration of the meaning appears difficult, often impossible. It is the very bases of reasoning which are deeply involved and irreversibly conditioned. But it is not only a matter of this. As regards orality and its characteristic as living globality, writing, and especially writing in the era of the mass printing industry, is the result of a mechanical editing, or a cold-blooded operation, separately laid out for the reader-interlocutors, with all the limits of a solitary vice which expects no reactions from its own audience, which moreover it does not know and which by all accounts would be unable to express its own reactions. One can interrupt, hiss, or applaud an orator. A writer one can only review. The secret neurotic substance of writing is all there. Montaigne was right, who clearly understood these things. "The book is an open letter sent to an unknown recipient."

Just by existing and functioning on a world scale, the mass media have put the book on trial. They have also put it in danger. It runs the risk of being rapidly made obsolete. When they pretend to advertise it, in reality they give it the kiss of death. They reduce it to a mere consumer good, a chocolate in cellophane. I have remarked elsewhere that the increasing insistence there is talk of libraries without books: microfilm and tapes are certainly less cumbersome, eliminate the problem of dust, can be more easily defended against damp. In a world which stakes—or seems to stake—everything on speed, miniaturization and immediate use have the future on their side. At what price? McLuhan's optimism, and Marcuse's too, both awaiting the gifts of high technology, is shown, on the eve of the year 2000, to be increasingly less well-founded. The foundations of human coexistence are slipping away. The everyday is losing its savor and the exceptional event is in crisis. Naturally, McLuhan can, not without a dash of coquetry, remove himself from severe criticism on this point by declaring himself a pure man of letters, wholly without a political sense and uninterested in value judgments that might go outside the properly technical level of the media. However, for Herbert Marcuse things are more complex: he cannot remove himself with similar arguments. The philosopher of world confrontation in 1968, the theorizer of one-dimensional man and the appeal to the excluded and marginal of the whole world as heirs of a working class integrated into the capitalist system and unmindful of its historic task in the construction of a different society, in which eros and efficiency can ultimately join together beyond the simplistic Freudian dichotomy between reality principle and pleasure principle, the question of technology and its large-scale effects are not a secondary question to be liquidated with a *bon mot*. I noticed, even before the explosion of 1968 and before the Paris students set up their barricades in May, along the Boulevard Saint Germain[21], that Marcuse, and with him all those technophiles who today—*sub specie technocratica*—are legion, was stuck and aligned on the old argument on the use of technique, which can be good or bad according to the macrosocial (ideological?) ends of which it makes use, independently of its effective functioning, empirically capable of being determined through conceptually directed and historically aware sociological research. It is a deeply contradictory reasoning, made suspect by "progressive" illusions. *Timeo Danaos et dona ferentes*.

NOTES

1. William Severini Kowinski, *The Malling of America* (New York: Random House, 1985), p. 51.

2. C. Freccero, "Massa e messaggio," *Tempo presente*, 55, July 1985 (my translation).

3. P. Zumthor, *La poèsie et la voix dans le civilisation médievale* (Paris: Presses Universitaire du France, 1984), p. 52.

4. *La Geste hilalienne*, ed. Lucienne Saada (Paris: Gallimard, 1985).

5. See, for example, Paul Thompson, *The Voice of the Past* (London: Pluto Press, 1978), Philippe Joutard, *Ces voix qui nous viennent du passé* (Paris: Hachette, 1983).

6. See my *Storia e storie di vita* (Laterza: Roma-Bari, 1982).

7. See, among others, the work of Pietro Crespi and Nuto Revelli.

8. This is the title of my recent *The Myth of Inevitable Progress* (Westport, CT: Greenwood Press, 1985).

9. Cf. in this respect, among others, G. Bettetini, "La spettacolarizzazione della realta," in *Il dopo McLuhan*, ed. G. Gamaleri (Pescara, 1981).

10. See my contribution "Historical Roots of Social Science," *Society* 22, no. 5 (July-August 1985): 15–17.

11. S. Acquaviva, "L'italiano incolto? Legge poco ma vede tanto," *Corriere della Sera*, 3 October 1985, p. 3.

12. See my (with collaborators) *Studi e ricerche sul potere*, 3 vols. (Rome: Ianua, 1980–83). More specifically, my *The myth of Inevitable Progress*, p. 156: "In contemporary terms, information means power. If power involves control, and if it is impossible to control what is not known, then information is the necessary, if not exclusive condition, which lies beneath every exercise of power."

13. James W. Carey, "Canadian Communication Theory: Extensions and Interpretations of Harold Innis," in G. J. Robinson and D. Theall, eds., *Studies in Canadian Communications* (Montreal: McGill University Programme in Communication, 1975), emphasis in text.

14. J. W. Carey, "Harold Adams Innis and Marshall McLuhan," *Antioch Review* 67, no. 1 (1967): 5–31; J. W. Carey and J. J. Quirk, "The Mythos of the Electronic Revolution," *The American Scholar* 39 (1970): 219–241, 395–424, nn. 2, 3.

15. Cf. especially Elihu Katz, Paul F. Lazarsfeld, *Personal Influence* (Glencoe, IL: Free Press, 1955).

16. Cf. my *La società come problema e come progetto* (Milan: Mondacori, 1979), chap. 8, "Gabriel Tarde—la societa come processo mimetico," pp. 158–183.

17. J. Baudrillard, *A l'ombre des majorités silencieuses* (Paris: 1982), emphasis in original.

18. For the criticisms levelled at Le Bon, especially by Freud, cf. my *Una teologia per atei* (Rome-Bari: Laterza, 1983), chap. 5 (English translation, New York: Associated Faculty Press, forthcoming).

19. J. Burckhardt, *La Civiltà del Rinascimento in Italia*, (Italian translation, Florence: Sansoni, 1921), pp. 153–154 (italics in original text).

20. B. Didier, *Stendhal autobiographe* (Paris: Presses Universitaire du France, 1983), p. 49. But for conceptually rigorous remarks, even though not protected against the risk of a psychologistic interpretation, see W. Dilthey, *Critica della ragione storica* (Turin: Einaudi, 1954) (Italian translation of *Gesammelte Schriften*, Teubner, Leipzig, Berlin, esp. p. 295 and pp. 302–310). As examples of autobiographies, Dilthey quotes those of St. Augustine, Rousseau, and Goethe.

21. Cf. the preface of my *Max Weber e il destino della ragione* (now published in the Biblioteca Universale, Laterza: Roma-Bari, 1985), pp. xvii–xli (English translation *Max Weber and the Destiny of Reason*, New York: Sharpe, 1982).

2

The Crisis of the Event: The Decline and Transfiguration of Charisma

THE "WHITE TRIBE" IN A MINORITY POSITION

In the world of systematic, functional interdependencies, the great event is useless. It is comparable to the archaeological dig of an expedition with little luck. We are still paying the price for the bravado of the nineteenth and early twentieth centuries when there was concern, in a very academic fashion, about what was history and what is not. The ambition was to arrive at the working-out of the pure concept of history, not unlike the way the alchemists proposed to isolate the philosophers' stone. There lay behind the theoretical concern, to be sure, the practical social one of ensuring a role and respectability for oneself by safeguarding the dignity and jurisdiction of the discipline. It is remarkable that this concern should still today find its subtle learned disciples. Niklas Luhmann writes:

Any reply to the question "How is social order possible?" must . . . be subdivided into different theoretical segments. The response might be: through meaning. One might say: through the formation of social systems which can maintain themselves for some time within stable boundaries in relation to a supra-complex environment. One could say: through socio-cultural evolution. Each of these replies illustrates as many instances of further work. However, a single question remains fundamental: the *problematic of a constituent unity of the discipline.*[1]

Possibly we should seek in this attitude at once scientific-impersonal and sociopolitical, the emotive basis and justifying *telos* which sustain the tension of the cultivated man, the *Kulturmensch*, and *Vir* of the great Western humanistic tradition, or that of the man in the full sense, and of the culture which is at once psychological structure, intellectual orientation, and sociopolitical platform. This culture essentially corresponds to an elitist attitude that seems incapable of any interest in the everyday. At most it recognizes for it, with condescension, a value as documentation, of folkloristic practice, ruled by the rhythms and repetitive modes of animal determination, shut off from invention, formula, or even simply appreciation of coherent systems of meaning. This culture does not, under present conditions, help progress towards human awareness. The symptoms of these limitations and the resulting impotence are obvious. For elite culture, of venerable classical-humanistic predominance, the modern triumph of the aesthetic-epiphanic moment is the surest sign of crisis, of insufficient historical stature, and cognitive-operational inadequacy. Once more it seems clear that men are ready for everything so as to avoid soberly confronting the objective difficulties of a real situation, that is, with the contradictions and conflictual conditions of their immediate, inescapable everyday life.

Even by not facing the difficulties of historical development in its current phase, one is ready to deny history. There is no doubt that within the theoretical framework of elite culture, the new historical culture appears absurd, senseless, without acceptable outlets. Elite culture feels itself besieged and understands that it is becoming a minority culture, which in its current forms is possibly condemned to irrelevancy. The idea I recently formulated regarding the white tribe,[2] which is certainly strong from the technical point of view, but demographically weak, might seem excessively pessimistic; but at the same time Pope John Paul II never tires of thundering, with moralistic invective at times worthy of the worst clerical reaction, against the "demographic suicide of Europe." Rather than the implacable defender of the right to life, possibly he spoke here in the first instance as the fervent Polish patriot, terrorized by the menacing danger of an invasion by Asians.

I have no difficulty in admitting that the formula sounds provocative. But if one looks calmly at the situations appearing on a world scale, it will not be hard to see that we are dealing with real questions. Moreover, a few months had gone by since the publication of my *Cinque scenari per il Duemila* (English tr. *Five Scenarios for the Year 2000*), where the formula appeared, and lo, in South Africa black uprisings exploded, blacks excluded by law from civil life. Not only this: there began to be cases of groups of blacks moving to the attack of European districts and white citizens who, barricaded in their houses, defended themselves with guns and machine guns. The siege is here. It is not a metaphor. It is a hard, precise reality. The whites cannot have too many illusions. At the end of the second millennium they find themselves superpowerful from the technical viewpoint, but in a clear minority and in danger of being pushed aside from as political and demographic point of view. To understand this situation, one must take a step back and pose some questions which might seem abstract.

For a start, one must clear about the most important fact in this twentieth century, now nearing its end. The most nat ural reply will probably be the great technical and organizational successes. The spectacular moon-landing will be remembered. The successes of the aerospace industry will be recalled. However, with a deeper analysis, it will not be hard to show that these technical successes, though undeniable, are all linked to earlier discoveries, for the most part due to the nineteenth century, which rather ungenerously is often pointed to as the "stupid century." From the electric light to the telephone, to radio and the great theories in physics that are the basis of the nuclear industry, the nineteenth century—especially in its last decades—gave a contribution of fundamental discoveries: especially if we bear in mind that it ended in a real, not simply chronological, sense with World War I, wherein the first, mortal blow to the European balance of power was inflicted, and in which towards the end, almost as a crowning glory, brought us to a cultural crossroads, so to speak, which gave birth to the great innovative intellectual trends. It is enough to think of the Vienna of the first years of this century and the discovery of psychoanalysis, twelve-tone music, modern linguistics, and the philosophy of language with the powerful support of the neo-positivist movement (Freud, Schönberg, Carnap). In comparison the twentieth century is poor in technical discoveries, while instead it is very rich in technico-practical applications of principles already acquired. The real novelty, the original importance of the twentieth century, must be sought in the social field. For the first time in history, it experienced two total world wars, involving both armies and civilian populations, and at the same time, an unheard-of historical fact; for the first time there come on stage as relatively autonomous and specific actors peoples and nations that up till then were present in history but without participating in it. They were present but in silence, waiting for their destiny to be decided by others. They were present as inert fuel, passive raw material, incapable of autonomous decisions and making history in the first person.

In this sense, the end of colonialism is not simply indicative of a new formal political layout. It is not only a matter of changing the names of some regions in Africa and Asia. We are in the presence of new protagonists in the historical process. With World War II there took place not only the sunset and end of Europe as strategic center of the world. Max Weber's complaint is more timely than ever: "World policy is no longer made in Berlin." One must only add, to complete the picture, that this policy is not even made in London or Paris, still less in Rome. With the removal of the governing elite of the United States from the East Coast establishment (from Boston and New York with Franklin D. Roosevelt and John F. Kennedy, to restrict ourselves to the last fifty years) to that, more recent and certainly rougher of the West Coast, or California, with Richard Nixon and Ronald Reagan, the very favored interlocutors themselves are changed. One looks further East, to Japan and the Pacific in general, rather than the Atlantic river and complicated Europe. A whole cycle of

civilization is ending. The diachronic historical process dominated by Western European culture, conceived of as the unique,
exclusive source of the great values which support human civilization, is dwindling. Following history as a diachronic process that moves from stage to stage in order to sum itself up
and recognize itself as in its highest and really "civil" stage,
in the Western way of life, predominantly Graeco-Roman-Ju-
daic-Christian, in its classical humanistic version, there is a
phase distinguished by the synchronic historical process, in
which all cultures are basically on the same level and interact
and confront each other according to their specific, and genuine, values.

This situation of cultural pluralism produces a state of ac-
tue unease among the holders of the monopoly of knowledge
and the groups in a position of relative privilege. Positions
dominant by long tradition, both in political and cultural terms,
both directly and vicariously, feel themselves threatened and
sense that history has changed its habitation. To the question
of how one should proceed in educating a native of Africa or
Asia, it is no longer possible to reply hastily as our illustrious
Marxist philosopher Antonio Labriola replied in the first years
of this century: "To begin with, I'd make him a slave." Clearly,
for the "native" to be a slave would have been the first step
in the long march of approaching European civilization, con-
oidored tho ultimato normative term, in principle coinciding
with the only thinkable human civilization and culture possible. It is not only that response, more than odd, which today
seems scandalous. The very question can no longer be put; it
is simply absurd. It is clear that for the holders of the monopoly of knowledge and its instruments the situation is rapidly
made dramatic. It involves blocking historical development and
confirming the monopoly of rationality, if only at the price of
restricting its area of validity. Examples and warnings have
not been lacking:

When Innis speaks of the monopoly of knowledge, as held by the
medieval church, this does not only refer to the ability of the church
to predict the future thanks to the prophets and astrologers, or to
collect in the monasteries the official knowledge of human experi-

ence. Rather, reference is made to the power of the church in producing a complete system of thought, an official vision of reality, by
way of the control of the word, of rituals, of the arts. The church
produced what we today would call a paradigm: a vision of the world
which predetermined what could be real, established the modes for
determining the truth in any explanation of the facts, even defined
what could be considered knowledge. The cultural monopoly of
knowledge was provided by the capacity to predetermine facts. The
present computer enthusiasts . . . may truly wish to share their
knowledge with everyone, but they are certainly not inclined to reject the technocratic vision which establishes what it is which establishes itself as an important fact. They do not want to monopolize
the data, but the approved model of thought, established, authorized,
the very definition of what is rational.[3]

At this point it is easy to understand why Western European
culture not only forbids the understanding of others: it even
prevents the *acceptance of the otherness of others*, their diversity, the difference of their traditions and habits of life. Hence
comes the risk today, linked to elite culture. Hence, further,
comes the attempt to theorize on the cultural plane, and on
the political plane to effect, the end of history. The crisis of
historicism finds in this its determining roots.

END OF HISTORY OR CRISIS OF ELITE HISTORICISM?

Meanwhile, a preliminary paradox should be noted: it is not
possible to perceive and understand the end of history without
an acute historical sensitivity. The real crisis of historicism is
not to be sought in internal polemics and in the various conflicting interpretive and conceptual currents into which this
extraordinary movement in nineteenth-century thought has
little by little broken up. The real crisis of historicism and the
dissolution of history that follows from it do not seem to me
caused by internal reasons, by conceptual deficiencies, or the
rise of purely intrinsic contradictions. They appear to me caused
by technico-scientific development at the moment this is
starting to generate itself and appear as an autonomous process, no longer needful of external approval nor legitimation.

Now it is necessary for historicism to discount everything which does not enter into its official canons, to excommunicate the other cultures and theorize the fence between history and the everyday. "Marginal" or "native" cultures are not cultures; they produce no meanings. They are only conditioned reflexes, automatic tropisms, repetitive practices, animal in their blind on-going and self-repetition, mechanically to infinity. The very evolution in a modernizing sense of the Third World is in this perspective attacked as spurious, essentially illegitimate, morally unacceptable. Progress and light are not given either for the Third World, separated in its purity from the technically advanced modern world, nor for the Third World that sets off, accepting change, as then this would involve only a graveyard of remains, a scrapyard of scanty cultural survivals, incongrously close to modern rational behavior. But how then can the theorizers of the end of modernity, to which they certainly do not deny analytic virtue or interpretive acuteness, respond? The end or the beginning of modernity? Or a provisional, distorted acquisition? Or new versions of it?

Arnold Gehlen must be interrogated. "The condition Gehlen calls post-historical" it has been authoritatively remarked,

does not only reflect . . . an extreme phase of development of technique, which we have not yet reached but may reasonably expect. Progress becomes routine also because on the theoretical plane the development of technology has been prepared and accompanied by the "secularization" of the very notion of progress. . . . The ideal of progress is empty, its final value that of producing conditions in which ever-new progress is possible. However, once the "whither" is removed, secularization becomes also the dissolution of the very notion of progress. . . . The "dissolution" of history . . . is moreover probably the character which most clearly distinguishes contemporary history as regards "modern" history. Contemporaneity . . . is that era in which, while with the perfection of instruments of information gathering and transmission a "universal history" would now be possible, precisely this has become impossible.[4]

Why is this? Let us leave aside the concept of secularization, a typical screening-concept, behind which one can put everything and nothing, due mostly to a misunderstanding of the famous Weberian *Entzauberung*. Let us also put aside the examination of Gehlen's thought, to which we shall be able to return later.[5] But why should the triumph of technology coincide with the end of history? One can agree that a certain notion of history, and culture, and way of life, and also of politics, may have entered in crisis with this, but why ever should this mean the end of history, of any history at all, its blocking, freezing, the de-historification of human experience?

These are not questions of a purely polemical kind or simple countercharge. Nor is it a matter of rhetorical tricks. The problem brought out by these authors is important. We have already pointed out earlier that whereas some scholars (A. Touraine, H. Marcuse), though different in their specific outlooks, nonetheless tend to converge when they see in communication, *débats*, verbal competence or *Kommunicativen Handeln*, the constituent fact of modern society, one should probably maintain that the capillary presence and impact of the mass media, along with the rapid computation of data and their transmission over distance in real time, are at the basis of phenomena which traditional Western culture is no longer able to master. Society comes to present itself as a *synchronic globality* differentiated and complex within, but still fundamentally unitary; fluid but at the same time bound to technicofunctional imperatives from which there is neither return nor escape, in that they are omnipresent and planetary. This globality, which expresses the simultaneous presence of all actors on the historical stage, through that itself postulating for them a real parity, makes a challenge to European culture to which this last, in its traditional terms of interior awareness, basically individualized, has no possibility of making an effective reply.

Systemic globality, simultaneous presence, horizonal flattening out, and hence, by necessity, interdependence of individuals, groups, and classes: the arrival of the masses meant only this, and it involved and involves this. It is not the end of the world. It is not the blockage of history. It is simply a different world that with difficulty comes into being. The common people come out of the catacombs, come out of the cellars of elite history, harshly, reveal their background, and ask for the right of citizenship *pleno iure*. The everyday requests the right of historical existence. This implies a radical change in the nature and method of procedure by historical development. European culture is not capable of fully understanding this change and does not have the instruments nencessary for accepting and explaining the history of those who have never had a history. European culture has been built on a basic duality of a classical kind, which not even Christianity could dent: on the one hand, man in the full sense, the beautiful and good; on the other, the many, the hoi polloi, those who do not make history, who can only suffer it.

This selective duality is intrinsic to European culture. It is its condemnation, the hallmark of its inferiority as regards the task. Unable either to accept or understand the new type of historical development, it denies it at the source, proclaims its end. But the synchronic age in itself does not mean, nor involves, the end of history. Elite culture is certainly in crisis. In the universe of the functional interdependence in which the individual is nothing else than the "surrounding of the system," it emphasizes the disappearance of the event and the decline of the man with charisma, the exceptional individual. Then it chooses, with doubtful courage, the abyss, the narcissistic anguish that weeps for itself. The pure event has been mythologized as the extra-everyday act which animates, rouses, and shakes the quiet, lazy flow of historical time. Regarding Cioran, it has been stressed with great insight that the extreme ritual of the superstition of the event, of the extraordinary act, is part of the "taste for ruin," and yet represents a final metaphysical point of honor:

If the idea of the inexorable seduces and sustains us, it is because it contains a metaphysical residue despite everything and represents the sole grasp we still have on a semblance of an absolute, without which no one can survive. One day, who knows, even this resource might disappear. At the apogee of our void we shall then be consecrated to the indignity of a complete wearing out, worse than an unexpected catastrophe, which is after all honorable, even prestigious. Let us be trusting, let us aim at catastrophe, more in keeping with our genius and our tastes.[6]

This romantic catastrophism expresses at once anguish and a sense of guilt, a taste for the purifying fire and also the need for a kind of extreme "military honors." History finishes and asserts itself, before this end, dramatic because it is also the end of the man we have known, in the sense that history can no longer begin again, that human planning as personal responsible personal initiative is impossible, that there is no longer a margin for a really human project; one, that is, not already taken for granted, since we have entered the realm of mechanical omni-calculability.

In reality it is to the machine and the universe of technology, this perfection without aim, that human responsibility is transferred, human only in taking the initiative, risking checkmate, and facing up to possible failure. Delegation to the machine and technique is banal, like science divorced from consciousness, like the order executed because it comes from above according to the pregiven hierarchical lines and is established by the regulations, cutting it off from its contents. The event is the discontinuity that checkmates and puts the well-oiled and sly balance of the system in crisis. But the event has disappeared from the historical horizon. The charismas have been dissolved. The means of quitting history can in fact be reduced to three, thereby declaring its end and decreeing its transformation into pure administration: (1) the universal systemic balance which, like a perfect utopia, excludes any possible change that is not the eternal return of the identical, and thus eternalizes the situation of the existing fact as an insurmountable *nec plus ultra*; (2) the aesthetic-epiphanic moment; (3) the mystic self-annihilating raptus which yearns and is consumed in the suicidal *cupio dissolvi*.[7]

THE LIMITATIONS OF EUROPEAN CULTURE IN A CULTURALLY PLURALISTIC WORLD SITUATION

The question of systemic balance sends us back inevitably to the critical analysis of systems theory in its now classical and traditionalist version, and its various incarnations by analysts of different cultural and political opinions. It will be taken up again in due course in order to establish its multiple interconnections: from Talcott Parsons's structural function- alism, still open on an historico-evolutionist angle, as witness the latest works of the Harvard sociologist, to the certainly more rigorous and extreme formulations by Niklas Luhmann of the social system as essentially self-referring system, and thereby impenetrably closed in its own logic. It has been cor- rectly observed that Luhmann means deliberately to abandon the old—historical and broadly humanistic—bases of sociolog- ical thought, as expressed in the works of the classics of the discipline. This is in order to establish it on relatively new bases, linked to general systems theory and the science of ad- ministration, profiting in this regard from, and drawing on, his professional experience as a former official in the admin- istration of lower Saxony in the Federal Republic of Germany. It is hard to avoid the suggestion that in his work, extraordi- narily provoking for traditional social scientists, above all be- cause of a language which yields in no way to the paleo-hu- manism of the classical type, Luhmann ends up by breaking every tie with gnoseological relativism in favor of a model of reified rationality, one that may, by pressing its premises to their logical conclusion, be ontological. It is clear we are deal- ing with an exit from history here, as well as a rejection of historicism; both deserve a detailed, concrete discussion. The logic of the homeostatic model, which seems to underlie these theoretical constructs even at their most ambitious (on the basis of which no change takes place that would cross the boundaries of the system) and which fails to postulate the re- turn to the conditions at the outset, also underlies its essen- tially ahistorical orientation.

As regards the aesthetic-demonstrative moment, it is diffi- cult to gainsay its essentially irrationalist inspiration. There is no doubt that it arises on the basis of a healthy dissatisfac- tion with the closed conception of rationality assigned to it by the traditions of the nineteenth century, which rests wholly on the calculation of the fit between the means available and the desired ends. The concept is devoted to the discovery of a monocausal connection, which duly pays for insufficiencies in approach and research techniques at the expense of the com-

plexity of the subjects investigated. At the same time, whereas
it worthily polemicizes against the overbearing thinking that
defines "appropriate" reality without occasionally seeing it as
embracing a corpse or a ghost, the aesthetic-demonstrative
moment on principle devalues values and experiences that
cannot enter its ephemeral theoretical framework, defined for
the purpose as "weak." It makes modernity, in the Western
European sense, coincide with the end of history and the dissolving of rationality.

It has been quite acutely remarked that "the difficulty encountered in distinguishing classical from ethnographic hermeneutics emerges as something different from a simple theoretical difficulty, and rather as a feature which is also itself
one of *destiny*," a remark which probably confirms an impassible limit. The quotation continues:

Just as the condition of radical otherness of other cultures appears
as an ideal, perhaps never realized and certainly not realizable for
us, so, in the proces of homologizing and contamination, the texts,
the "classics" in the literal sense, belonging to our tradition and which
our humanity has always been measured against, progressively lose
their cogency as models. They too enter the great dry dock of survivals. Anthropology, like hermeneutics, is neither the encounter with
radical otherness nor the scientific systematizing of the human phenomenon in terms of structures. It probably falls back into its dialog
form, into the only way in which the *arkhè* can appear in the epoch
of completed metaphysics—the form of survival, of marginality, and
of contamination.[8]

The image of the "dry dock of survivals" is certainly captivating, if not downright seductive. It is true that in the epoch
of the decline of the great global ideological constructs, convinced they held the key to the laws of historical development
but basically void of specific empirical contents, Nietzsche's
"garden of history" can easily lead us to think of the store of
theatrical costumes, where the mask and the disguises do not
seem to correspond to any strong, precise, stable identity. But
if this identity is produced by the globalization of technical
procedures, and if this process contains a compelling, basically unitary logic, is there not in the very idea of the "dry

dock of survivals" of the "storehouse of masks" an internal contradiction which covers up the confusion between weak causality and temporo-cultural discontinuity?

The conception of Western European culture as the sole norm or source of values above and beyond any other form of culture, produced by human groups on a world scale, appears disarmed before the current historical situation where hitherto unheard-of cultures and hitherto excluded peoples enter personally onto the stage of international life and politics. It can neither hold up against, nor confront, the challenge of the exception in rational, intersubjective terms, nor accept an historical development in which its values are not on principle considered dominant ones. The sole solution to the emergency caused by the entrance of new peoples into history now lies essentially in entrusting oneself to the man of providence or charismatic leader.

CHARISMA AS THE EXTRAORDINARY, PERSONALIZED RESPONSE TO THE "CHALLENGE OF THE EXCEPTION"

It is not by chance that in Western culture studies and interpretations of charisma should precisely center on the prevailing conception of the great man who makes history, in the classico-humanist tradition. It is suggestive that this tradition has not been damaged, but rather reinforced, by the Christian, especially Pauline, tradition, to which Max Weber, among modern sociologists, refers.[9] In this context, it is scarcely necessary to remark that charisma reinforces and supremely justifies and confirms the counterposing of history to the everyday. In fact, for the most part, charisma has been studied and analyzed, as the personal attribute of an extraordinary individual. This could also help to explain why even serious and generally well-documented and careful scholars should have been able to fall into the gross confusion between charismatic leader, in the true prophetic-religious sense, and the great man or leader of the political kind.[10] Taking charisma as an essentially personal attribute makes the concession, on a more or less broad scale, to psychologizing tendencies aimed at dismissing institutional-structural problems as states of mind or psychic worries, seem inevitable. In reality, charisma does not appear in a social void. It needs a precise historical horizon even if it then denies this and proclaims the end of history. It presents itself first as an inter-individual relation. For this reason the followers are at least as important as the charismatic leader. From this viewpoint, we can grasp a further limitation. The distinction between the religious-prophetic charismatic leader and the great man of a broadly cultural and historical type is at stake; one can subsume easily the category of charismatic Carlyle's hero, and thereby the humanistic, paleo-humanist, Plutarch-style conception of historical development, as well as eliminating Emerson's "oversoul" and Nietzsche's *Übermensch*, which find their exact counterpart in Weber's *Kulturmensch*. The limitation also concerns the elitist, aristocratic, and individualist conceptions that are not effectively able to explain or even take account of, interpret, and describe the relation, the irreducible reciprocity, between the leader and the mass of followers, apostles, faithful, or true believers.

A purely passive role, it seems, is reserved for the latter—almost that of fuel supply, awaiting the flame from above. In classical antiquity, this conception is at the basis of the "lives of famous men," presented for edification, as Plutarchian exemplars or *enkomia*. However, this leaves unilluminated the basic problematic point; the relational dialectic between leader, followers, and the community derived therefrom. Rather than of a charismatic leader one should speak of a charismatic community. Max Weber's limitations seem obvious in this regard—and insurmountable. Probably they sink their roots in Weber's own biography, the links with his family and the cultural and political climate of the Germany he lived in.[11] Moreover, Weber himself, with great honesty, recognized that he was a child of the bourgeoisie and thus placed himself historically and politically, as every aware social researcher is bound to do. What is striking is that in the face of the dilemma of each modern democracy on the eve of European fascisms—or democracies with a broadened social base or *Führerdemokratie*—it did not even hypothetically occur to Weber to think seriously about the former alternative. Before the crisis of legal bureaucratic power, unable to confront positively the exceptional, unforeseen situation, Weber could only invoke the man endowed with extraordinary gifts, those "grace" had inspired. This person's exploits depended on the specific historical context and the attitude of the followers themselves. An irrational and tendentially metahistorical way out, only exceptionally does the charismatic leader seem capable of positive and lasting solutions. The solution of his activity as the great crowd charmer, ever-needful of "confirmation" and at all events unsuited to rationally provide for his succession, generally appears as a traumatic one, often with tragic implications.[12]

Recently, an example of similar results can be seen in the vicissitudes of the Californian sect, The People's Temple, led by the Rev. Jim Jones. Elsewhere I have dwelt on this case, which has taken on a symbolic value from the mass suicide in Guyana that sealed its destiny.[13] This involves a sect which on the one hand, while wishing to win proselytes, did not manage to establish a tolerable contact with the outside world, and on the other hand had no other recourse than to sum itself up, and lose itself, in its leader: the Rev. Jones himself, obeying him to the point of self-annihilation. However, examples in this regard may be found in the present both in the context of the great positive religious and in the spread of those aggregations known as new religious movements: a various, synthetic magma derived from different theoretical and cultural moulds. For example,in the context of Roman Catholicism there has been long discussion of the importance and of the space occupied by the neo-charismatics, otherwise known as the neo-pentecostals, or "Movement for the Renewal of the Spirit." Beyond the diversity of interpretations and individual evaluations, it is universally recognized that these groups have an essentially emotional, irrational character, where their leader has a recognized role and is a constant point of reference.[14]

More recently, still in the context of the Catholic Church, Opus Dei has made the headlines: founded in 1928, it is an institution with the declared aim of confronting the spread of

Marxism and the related danger of de-Christianization.[15] An
object of raging disputes and controversies, lauded or feared,
Opus Dei has been attacked and denounced for its integralist
spirit, its sectarian methods, and its extreme authoritarian-
ism employed internally. Such terms were used, (and by a
Christian publishing house like Claudiana) as "stifling au-
thoritarianism" an "unembarrassed morality of the end justifying the means," "unalloyed use of lying and psychological
terror," "medieval practices of self-punishment" and brainwashing. The text of the press release in which Klaus Steigleder's book on Opus Dei was presented reads thus:

It is clear that Opus Dei needs to get its subjects at a tender age so
as to be able to mould them at its pleasure, maintaining them also
as adults in a condition of constant dependency on the figure of the
"Father" (or Director), while being concerned with men and women
the Institution is to introduce into key posts in the highest sectors of
society and public life.

That this is not a matter of excessive or tendentious interpretations is moreover to be seen in the words of the founder,
Escriva' de Balaguer: "Free man, submit to voluntary slavery" (Cammino, 761).

Do not desire to be an adult. A child, always a child, even if you
were dying of old age.—When a child stumbles and falls, no one is
surprised (. . .), its father runs to pick it up. When an adult stumbles and falls, the first impulse is to laughter. . . . Your sad everyday experience is full of obstacles and falls. What would happen to
you if you were not ever more a child? Don't want to be an adult. A
child, and when you stumble, the hand of your Father-God raises you
up (Cammino, 870).

Infancy, far from being a transitory phase in the individual's development, is taken as the basic datum for erecting a
state of dominance by superiors, and which thrives on the sense
of guilt, tension, and inadequacy of the subjects: as I remarked, this is a climate not unlike what we find in some
religious sects or new movements.
    Aside from the demands which clearly lie at the base of

these ferments and which are the cement of the creation of these groups, and contribute to their spreading and consolidation (the desire to give of oneself on the affective and intellectual level, the search for wholeness, coherence, truth, and meanings), one must additionally stress their sectarian spirit and absolute intransigence. One stresses too their intolerance, generally linked to a proselytizing drive, and acquiescence in the commands of a charismatic leader—characteristic traits of a large part of modern charismatic movements, diffused in the West in our days.[16]

SECTS AS DISPENSERS OF CERTAINTY IN AN UNCERTAIN WORLD

Faced with the state of complexity and consequent uncertainties in the contemporary world, the sects seem to offer clear, unequivocal solutions, precise supports, rules of prohibition, and absolute certainties. An incontestable source of the division between good and evil, and of approval and disapproval in these groups is the charismatic leader, whose authority is absolute and generally reinforced by the confirmation of the specific gifts he possesses: from the gift of tongues to the power of healing, from the ability to read consciences to the power of prophecy, from levitation to the ability to astrally project. The guru's and the charismatic leader's magnetism and ascendency thus acquire an ever-increasingly decisive role of an absolutist stamp, to the point of arriving at the submission of their disciples in every varied aspect of their existence. The itineraries may be different, the methods, multiple, but the tendency generally is just one: starting from a series of real needs and difficulties, the desire to seek, the desire to give oneself, and the need for self-abnegation—characteristics of much of the world of youth—a certain leader (applying himself and delegating to others specific recruiting and educational techniques) creates a following that gradually comes to be reinforced through an almost total control of the members.

If this process is clear and obvious in its dramatic aspects as regards the case of Jim Jones's church, the People's Temple, it is not thereby lacking in other religious groups that have achieved a wide following in our own times, with relative advantages and disadvantages. It is true that the alteration of states of consciousness produced by a certain type of meditation can lead to a better psycho-physical integration, to a raising of creativity and intelligence, and the full expounding of one's own potentialities, as Transcendental Meditation promises. It is equally true that the Maharishi—the undisputed Indian charismatic leader—sets the goals and propounds programmatic points (among these, the "intensification of the successes of governments" and "the bringing to fulfillment of the economic aspirations of the individual and society," naturally leaving aside the question of the type of government and society). He is at the summit of the decidedly pyramidal type of organizational form which brings Transcendental Meditation to a common position with many other movements of a religious-charismatic stamp. Physical distance and the difficulty an individual meditator has just in being able to see the Maharishi from afar only increase the fascination of this charismatic leader, portrayed in white clothing, a flower grasped in his hands, whose priestly image and voice are multiplied through the use of videotape, whose words are borne from the teacher in simultaneous translation—part of a fluid organizational chain that runs from the guru to the national leader, arriving at the regional leader, the course leader, and finally at the meditator. The contents diffused certainly do not have the negative evidence we find in other cases; however, a critical vision of the modern world and science is discouraged. On the contrary, there is encouragement of abandonment to the charismatic leader, along with the adoption of a consequent, more correct, view of the world through a progressive acculturation and initiation, progresive abandonment of any social commitment save through the teaching and the development of the technique of mediation (there would, that is, be no more reason for conflict if employer and workers were meditators). And there is always and at all events adoption of the opinion of one's leader.

In the case of the Children of God, who have as their charismatic leader Moses David, and more generally of the Jesus

Family, one may speak of techniques like that of flirting-fishing for the recruitment of followers. And, with the followers of Rajneesh, we have the exaltation of sex as means of groups cohesion and consolidation of the organizational structure (a technique specific also to the People's Temple). By contrast, in the case of Transcendental Meditation, ISKON (or Hare Krishna) and also the Moonies, sex is regarded as a means to be employed solely for purposes of procreation. In the book *I nouvi monaci*,[17] there is a description of the conception of marriage, procreation, and death, current and spread throughout the Hare Krishnas. In the movement, women are considered as an "inferior being, of little intelligence, weak and lustful," who must thus be "protected and guided," in that this is a matter of a constant "source of danger," as well as of "a serious obstacle along the path of spiritual realization." Through a gradual process of estrangement from the culture of origin, and constant re-socialization, this and similar messages are now a common heritage among the groups that referred to his Divine Scripture Baktivedanta Swami Prabhupada, and which are now led by his North American successor. He, moreover, in a meeting held on 28 May 1985 in Via di San Simone in Rome, explained how science should be followed as long and only as long as it does not enter into conflict with God. Had science perhaps made anyone happier? In reality, we must be aware that science is not capable of guiding humanity, can tell us nothing about the most important aspects and problems, for example, death. If it is true that there are those who complain about sects, who speak about brainwashing, it is also true that these same people do not seem to take into account how sience has misled people, or how it has had the result of leading us to "mechanical reductionism." It would thus be true science to free oneself from the passions and from ignorance, with the hope of the charismatic leader. In this perspective, the body and its needs should be firmly re-positioned. "The oyster's shell is ugly, the pearl is beautiful." For the follower, therefore, the body is not beautiful: indeed, beneath the skin it is decidedly ugly. The soul, the consciousness which comes from the soul, is beautiful. Consequently, whoever loves the good loves Krishna and his teaching: he stops killing and eating flesh, to avoid becoming wicked ("you are what you eat"). He uses sex only for purposes of procreation ("and for what else? That is its real purpose, and you must use things for what they have been made for." Moreover, "if sex makes people happy, why is everyone unhappy?").

In these cases, continual daily work, uprooting from the culture of origin, the elimination of external influences, the use of special diets, and the discouraging of a deep relation with a partner and strong concentration on the charismatic leader can lead to a total, acritical acceptance of the ideology of the group, the directives delivered from above, and the message of the charismatic leader. Good internal organization, recourse in some cases to means of mass communication, the prestige the group draws from certain memberships or the halo of martydrom and unmerited persecution in other cases, and their strong economic power, can be further reasons for motivation and reinforcement.

THE "CHILDREN OF MOON," OR THE BUSINESSMAN AS PROPHET

We may take as an example of a strongly structured sect that of the followers of Sun Myung Moon. The movement's publicist speaks of the founder as someone who "has not studied theology or philosophy" but who has, however, been chosen "by God to express His will." Revelation is said to have occurred by degrees, from when he was sixteen. From that time Moon is said to have tried "to give a reply to the fundamental questions in life and the universe,"—not without difficulty, if he had to "overcome enormous obstacles." Indeed, "seeking the truth he has spend a life of suffering and bitter battles against the forces of evil," sustained in his difficult journey by communication with God and the saints. Part of the teaching imparted in the *Principles*,[18] the basic text of the movement, is the re-presentation of the theme of the Fall, with an interpretation that shifts away from those of Genesis. So, it is recorded that

The sin of the angel was a sin of fornication. As one cannot commit fornication alone, there must have been someone who sinned with him. But who could it have been? The Bible tells us about only three beings who committed a sin in the garden of Eden: the serpent, Adam and Eve.

The interpretation provided by Moon and the movement inspired by him is that "Adam and Eve betrayed God, their true father, and joined Satan, the false father." This means that "even if Eve and the angel committed fornication concretely by means of their spiritual bodies, in fact children cannot be born of a relation between a human being and an angel. At any rate, Eve inherited Satanic 'love,' so that whem Adam and Even had their relation, which, naturally, produced children, it was inspired by Satanic 'love' and their children were born from this love: hence all men are children of Satan."

Satan is thus supposed to have improperly played the part of the Lord, whereas the latter is said never to have been able to "have the central role in any of the events of the world, nor to govern it according to His will alone." Hence the fall, spiritual and physical, and the need for the coming of the Messiah. Except that: "tragically . . . the chosen, prepared people failed in recognizing the Messiah when he came," and Jesus was crucified, against the divine intention. "The death on the cross was not the mission God had originally prepared for Jesus, His son. Rather, it became the painful secondary dispensation of God, made necessary by the lack of faith of the Jewish people," rather than by the failure of John the Baptist, himself responsible for "lack of faith" and "ignorance." Hence, then, arose the need of a "second Coming, which is to be realized in there, "the Last Days." Days, that is, that require the coming together of "all the faithful of the different religions," who "are destined to unite around the Lord of the Second Coming."

Once Adam and Eve's mission had failed, originally destined to realize the ideal of unity with God, a different Trinity must now be re-established "centered on the Heart and the ideal of God." Hence arises the function of a second Adam and a second Eve. "True spiritual Parents," and hence the presence of the Lord of the Second Coming, who comes "as a True Father" to establish the Trinity "spiritually as well as physically." He is coming, after a long period of preparation, of which the conflict between religion and philosophy is part, as well as a "vision of life like Cain's." Under this heading one should consider rationalism (Descartes), empiricism (Locke, Bacon), deism (Herbert), the Hegelian left (Strauss, Feurebach), and Marxism (Marx, Engels, Lenin). Against this, there is the "vision of life like Abel's," with pietism (Spencer), Methodism (Wesley), the Quakers (Fox), the great religious revival in America (Edwards), and German idealism (Kant, Fichte, Schelling, Hegel). Now, the situation is supposedly favorable to a Second Coming:

The attacks which the world of the Cain type, the Satanic side, launches against the Abel-type world, the heavenly side, constitute the process of restoration. The Abel type, from the heavenly side, establishes the foundation for good through his own sacrifice. The ultimate struggles must occur to repair, through payment of damages, on a world scale, the killing of Abel by Cain. Cain's world strikes Abel's first, but the result is that Abel's world wins the victory over Cain's—even if for this to happen it will probably be necessary to pass through a Third World War.

But when, where, will Christ return? He will return shortly, in the present era, since, as is evident from many signs, these are the Last Days. Certainly not in Israel, however, not among the people which is already stained by His killing and responsible for the failure of the plans for salvation desired by God. The nation chosen for this second decisive Coming is, rather, Korea, as the scriptures—correctly interpreted—show. The qualifications of the chosen nation imply in fact that it should have had "experiences of suffering similar to those of God," that it should have "many religions" in its heart, and represent "the line of conflict between God and Satan," something the geographical and political position of Korea has made inevitable. It should have had "a period of national indemnity," between the seat of "messianic prophecies"; and as we have seen, it is Korea that has given birth to Moon, here that he has had, progressively, the revelation of truth and of his mission in the world.

On this fragile theoretical base, of a syncretic type, Sun Myung Moon has constructed a real empire. The Spiritual Association for the Unification of the Christian World, or SAUCW, originates the Moon's teaching, which all sources let it be understood is the new Messiah, sent by the Lord for the salvation of mankind, after the failure of the same mission by Jesus Christ.

We know Sun Myung Moon was born in 1920. However, the biographical details, as happens for the majority of the charismatic leaders of these new movements appear, at least as concerns the first part of their lives, vague and contradictory, shrouded in a certain air of mystery. In fact this increases the fascination of the charismatic leader, who it may be supposed has had to deal with ideological enemies, hostile to him and to his mission because of the special gifts he bears, and the message embodied in him. Once these difficulties have been overcome, we find the Reverend Moon now head of a flourishing association, born in 1954 in Seoul, which has developed on a world scale, taking on hierarchical implications and mostly relying on a base of young people. Each member is followed, wherever he goes, by a spiritual father or mother (the "perfect family" is the model continually presented): each family is guided by a leader, as is every country or region, up to the supreme head, Sun Myung Moon. The missionary spirit pervading the association, which is translated into constant attempts at proselytizing, has over the years borne its fruits, if it is true that Moon controls a series of periodical publications (also daily newspapers in the United States), and that his financial empire is flourishing. There is talk of millions of dollars, and the movement has been defined from many sides as "a begging multinational." It includes real estate investments, but also profitable commercial enterprises that, together with the takings from the unpaid work of the members and their contributions, allow, added to the product of begging, the financing of prestigious cultural initiatives.

Thus the presence of scholars and scientists of undisputed reputation is invited to discuss subjects of general interest, of real importance, with the aim of Moon's greater glorification and that of his movement, devoted to the subject of peace, interdisciplinary studies, and the struggle against drugs, terrorism, and deviance. The organizations and branches of the movement are various, used according to the moment and circumstances, aside from the specific context concerned: from the Universal Movement for the Search for Universal Values to the International Cultural Foundation, the International Federation for Victory over Communism to the New ERA. This last, the New Ecumenical Research Association, is concerned with the promotion of ecumenical research through research, conferences, and publications. In a time of ecumenicism it is easy to present it as a laudable initiative, one to be encouraged. Thus scholars really interested in the subject and of a conciliar and ecumenical spirit generally take part, perhaps without being fully aware of it, in what becomes a movement of reinforcement of the prestige of Moon's movement, which presents itself in cultural guise, above sectarian and partisan interests. Clearly this involves, aside from anything else, an increased identity and self-esteem for the members of a group so well-known and committed in an ethical and universal sense. It also in addition involves a growth of prestige for Moon, supreme head of the movement, undisputed charismatic leader, photographed alongside Nobel prize winners, decorated with honarary degrees, certified in some way by the sciences with a mechanism set in motion, and similar in many ways, by the Maharishi for Transcendental Meditation.

The PWPA (Professors' World Peace Academy), moreover, lives up to its name. Now present in 90 countries, it manages to finance academic projects (and everyone knows academics are underpaid), organizes seminars and conferences, and makes use of the names of people eminent in the field of culture, such as Morton Kaplan on the international level, to Vincenzo Cappelletti, of the Enciclopedia Italiana, at the Italian. These remarks do not exhaust the intensity of the initiatives and undertakings which spread out from Moon and return to him. Investigated on many occasions about his supposed links with the South Korean secret information services (KCIA), close, at that time, to Richard Nixon, accused of plagiarism and of exploitation of his followers, imprisoned for tax evasion in the States, Moon seems to have overcome the worst period of his misfortunes. Today he is at the center of the movement he founded, where together with his latest wife, he is pointed out as the "True Parent," the prototype of the Happy Family.

FROM ABSOLUTE OBEDIENCE TO SALVATION

Moon's followers, who have been present for many years in Italy, live an ascetic life of great commitment and labor, wherein meditations on the Father's words alternate with work for the common good, raising money in the name of unspecified "lay missionaries," and proselytizing. The Moonies hand over all their earnings to the organization, work for nothing in Moon's commercial undertakings (among the best-known is the world trade in ginseng), and collect funds. The *Washington Times* ("the alternative voice of the world's most important capital"), which in its first three years of life cost Moon a hundred million dollars in losses, published on 11 July 1985 the results of an inquiry by Senator Orrin Hatch on Moon, and, thereafter, the testimonies favorable to the Reverend. A follower of Moon will thus be able further to convince himself on the goodness of his charismatic leader, unjustly investigated and condemned, persecuted (like Jesus Christ) because of his commitment to others; and his faith in and devotion towards the charismatic leader are reinforced. Moreover, for many, membership in Moonie groups presents undoubted advantages: youths who could never otherwise have done so can travel and get to know other countries, with different manners and customs, come in contact with young people of other nationalities, fill important positions, and contact university professors, newspaper editors, and politicians, otherwise unapproachable. In exchange, absolute obedience and conformity to the teachings and sayings of the charismatic leader are required.

Moon's speeches are reported with great prominence in the movement's press (for Italy, see the review *La Nuova Era*, now in its eleventh year of life). This press continually re-presents the paternal, smiling image, that of the spiritual guide close and affable. He is generally flanked by his wife, his neck garlanded with multicolored flowers. His words, inspired by concern, solicitude, and affection towards the latest, most insignificant follower, are reported. The luck the latter has in being connected with "Real Parents" is stressed.

When will God be able to become the true God? Only when men will have True Parents through whom he can start to build a true world in which divine love is respected. Now, we who are false children can be grafted onto those who are real children and thus create the whole human family. This is why fallen man needs the Messiah as his saviour.[19]

Contacts with Moon's followers and reading of internal publications point to proselytism and propaganda against the outside world as fundamental doctrines deriving from the Universal Principles and word of Moon. Other doctrines include the disciples' commitment to battle the devastating effects of the modern world, such as feminism, violence, and spreading communism, and their struggle to build a better world. The Moonie slogans stress the failure of new social forms such as open marriage, hippie communes, and the various types of living together which are not that of the happy family, united in belief in the Universal Principles, modelled on Moon's example. For a full realization of his own mission, the follower will then leave his original family, reinforce his own ties with the group, spend his own days in working or begging activities for the movement, by order, in a city not that of his birth or where he has lived, in such a way that the process of uprooting and re-socialization can be carried on with less resistance and difficulty. The young people see a life of sacrifices and self-denial proposed for them, but in the service of a great ideal, a life of heroism, where they probably had lived on the margins of cultural and social life. Unfortunately there are no adequate investigations of the socio-economic and cultural origins of the movement's members; from the results of partial enquiries made into these and other similar groups, one may, however, imagine that the movement rests on petty and middle bourgeois strata, at middle and middle-to-low cultural levels.

As has been noted, total and acritical acceptance of the word of the charismatic leader, Moon, is part of the member's life: source of wisdom, loved (and hated by his enemies), precisely because of his mission, his role as messenger, Messiah. Thus, in this perspective it will not be surprising if it is no longer the individual who decides his own life, his choices, his future: indeed, this is a matter of responsibilities delegated to his own leader, in the last analysis to Moon, source of certainty and salvation, charismatic leader by antinomasia.

So also an important act like the choice of a partnenr for life is delegated to Moon, who in a massive assembly of followers pairs strangers and joins them in matrimony. Thus in *Today's World*[20] there is talk of the Blessed Family, and the fact is repeated that a husband and wife who work together are, like Jesus Christ, joined to the Holy Spirit, as their day is exclusively dedicated to purposes of salvation. For these same purposes it may moreover happen to a young couple that they separate as soon as they have been married, for some days, months, or even years, for the greater glory of God. However, as God's plans are revealed to Moon, it is good that he be the one to identify the most suitable partner, bless marriages, stress the good fortune (if not the necessity) that their first commitment should be to the true church, and encourage them because they are already on the good road of brotherhood and the realization of a "true family." If the imposing of a partner contrasts with the usually accepted stereotypes of contemporary society, that happens precisely because of the typical deficiencies and distortions of the world we live in. Salvation is laid down in obedience to the Word of the new Messiah, in the acceptance of the orders given by him, and in alignment with the model he has proposed.

THE TV POPE

However, charisma is self-defeating. It seeks refuge in nothingness. The crisis of the event and the dissolution of charisma would in themselves seem good opportunities for positively transcending current difficulties and for trying for an essential legitimation of power. But here the decline and final checkmate of charisma, instead of opening up new possibilities in terms of broadening the historical perspective, open up a leaden phase of despair. Elite culture does not resign itself. It perceives in charisma a way out, the alternative to the widening of the social bases of the socio-political regime. But this alternative does not stand up; it seems eaten away by a mysterious law of entropy. Charisma cools. A disturbing paradox arises. At the moment when it seems easiest for the charismatic leader to manipulate his followers as he pleases, when they are reduced to a jelly-like mass, it is the leader himself, the holder of the charisma, on whom grace has bestowed its gifts, who proclaims a certain degree of failure. The leader is diminished. The mass media are the vehicle for his image. They follow his journeys and tireless apostolic efforts, but here their constant, hammering barrage seems to defeat and in some strange way flatten and annihilate the same august personage whom they ought to diffuse and exalt. Charisma, besieged by the mass media, is routinized and becomes predictable and banal. The holy suffering face of the leader-pastor loses its aura. The pastoral staff becomes a prosaic walking stick. The halo melts off the charismatic leader. He is coopted, made smooth and homogenized, taken for granted.

Once, the charismatic could plausibly make one think of an innovative force, if not a revolutionary dynamo. The old testament prophet stated, emblematically, "It is written . . . but I say unto you." He reversed the rule and conventional wisdom. A new era began. He announced the good news.

Today's charismatic is coopted by the logic of the mass media. He cannot escape their conditioning. He is transformed into a consumer-good. As a highly instructive example, consider the Pope's intercontinental trips. John Paul II arrives, descends the plane's steps, prostrates himself to kiss the ground. It is a beautiful, suggestive gesture. But, repeated tens of times, it is diluted and loses its symbolic force.[21] It declines from a symbol to being a mere sign, a mechanical gesture. The revered guest becomes a caricature: "Here he is again!" It seems clear the Pope wants to reach his people. He wants to see them face to face, directly, without mediations, even after the assassination attempt in St. Peter's Square that nearly cost him his life. He wants to see his people close to, touch their hands, look them in the eye. This is not an intellectual Pope like the tormented, subtle Montini Pope. This is a fighting Pope, one from the trenches; the Polish church has been at war for almost half a century with its political regime. However, between the Pope and the people of God there is the TV. The famous "two-step flow of communication" theory of Paul F. Lazarsfeld is here paradoxically inverted. According to Lazarsfeld, between the means of mass communication and the individual there was the small primary group, a valuable filter with an anti-manipulative function. Here, on the contrary, the TV is strategically placed between the Pope and his people: a selective filter and at the same time a powerful curtain capable of performing maskings, producing reactions, and portentous reversals. In fact, the people as totality, the real, living mystical body, what the Pope must choose as his ideal interlocutor as living Church, is not reached and does not seem attainable. Televisual communication is "cold." It concedes nothing. Before everything, it serves itself.

There is no doubt Karol Wojtyla—Pope John Paul II—has an eye and an ear for the means of mass communication. They do not intimidate him. What by his own admission happened to the American Democratic Presidential candidate, Walter Mondale, cannot happen to the Pope. Mondale came out with a stiff, haggard face. The television "plastered" him. He was not only "encumbered": the television "cadaverized" him. From the screen there descended towards—or rather, there etched itself on—the spectators an unreal figure, a mannikin, with glassy eyes and disjointed gestures. This certainly cannot be said of Wojtyla, who has the broad sweep of the consummate actor, the lively glance that seems to look into the depths of each of the hundreds of thousands of the faithful, the certainty that makes him occupy the center stage with extreme naturalness. Aside from his natural gifts, he is helped by his youthful experience as an actor. And yet something does not work. The charisma of the sacred, which should issue forth from the Pope's form and gestures, seemed to be filtered and impoverished by the screen. Despite the informed strategy undertaken in the use of the media, the religious significance of the encounters of the Pope with the crowd to which he seems to devote himself with such urgent haste does not emerge clearly. The sacred comes out subtly desacralized. The mediation of the TV has a price probably higher than anyone could have predicted.

The relation with the Pope is not direct, but mediated by the TV. This mediation has results which should be investigated in depth. Television charisma has nothing prophetic about it any more. The religious declines into the bureaucratic; the sacred, into the theater. As regards television, when it apparently places itself at the service of the evangelical message and the papal apostolic mission, in reality it serves itself, obeys its own internal logic, engulfs, reduces, and translates into its language of images every other discourse.

It has been remarked that

the television Pope belongs to the world beyond the screen (as regards the mass of the people), a superior reality, a stronger one we could define as "hyper-reality," endowed with greater power than the flat reality of the everyday. This reality is a new form of the sacred, as a place of collective meta-signification. . . . However, it involves a sacred very different from the catholic one. Rather than making up the invisible foundation of visible reality, it is the representation of another reality parallel to the ordinary one, experientially present but not attainable. One goes there daily and one does not need to interrupt everyday temporality for it, as for the catholic sacred; it is familiar, and one can always refer to it, establish a contact. Just switch on the TV. The sacred of the great pilgrimages was reached with great difficulty, after covering kilometers of road or impassible paths. The television sacred is very close and familiar. Close, even if not fully attainable. It remains a separate reality, like the sacred in general. Here, the separateness is given by the screen. It is not possible to go beyond the border of the sacred-non-sacred, as the screen prevents you from going inside, into the heart of the sacred. It is very near but not approachable further.[22]

The television sacred is thus a horizontal one, which does not imply transcendence and lacks vertical depth. The television medium destroys any ritualization, the sense of the "people of God" and the mystical body. The multiplicity of dots, of banal individuals as users-consumers, predominates. The sacred is commodified. From religiosity one moves on to church religion, holder of the monopoly over the precious merchandise called sacred. The tension between sacred annd religious, sacred and market, drops. One produces advertising for the Pope's visit, as for diapers and detergent. The community of the faithful has disappeared into the blur of the undifferentiated public of TV viewers. The remote control, not the prayer, is the new channel towards the sacred and the divine. But this channel inverts the relationship; it is not the individual's reality that moves towards the sacred, but the sacred that becomes "individualized," like a coat cut to measure and literally "profaned."

Yet the TV Pope is encircled by an aura, artifically created, of triumph. Like a mythic hero, he sets off to seek the golden fleece, or the loyalty and obedience of men and women in distant lands, so as to ensure their salvation, after undergoing and overcoming tests of unbelievable difficulty. The TV Pope, it has been acutely remarked, although head of a universal church, is really a charismatic leader without followers, a man of the crisis who tries his crossing of the desert. But he is not wholly alone. In fact the lenses of the TV camera are following, capturing his every gesture, word, aspect, and (in this case at least) present themselves as witnesses and at the same time as representatives of the whole of humanity.[23] The confirmation of the extraordinary gifts of the charismatic leader, Weber's famous *Bewährung*, is not to be sought in the peace achieved or the universality of the religious credo recognized by the new proselytes, but rather the very fact of the ceremony, the mass spectacle that the television transmits, multiplies and "invents." Not the Pope but the TV is at the center of interest. The Pope is only an actor among others, with the crowd, and the landscape. Guizzardi acutely remarks:

The crowds gathered by the charismatic leader will never seriously mobilize, neither to follow their leader nor to defend their faith in the real sense. In fact, mobilization is a goal in itself, as this enthusiasm already corresponds to utopia; the celebration of unity in the ceremony is none other than the symbolic but real celebration of a now attested ability to overcome the crisis. For the mass media and especially the TV, the proof lies precisely in the fact of determining if the charismatic leader will manage to unite the crowds and lift them up in enthusiasm. This and not his words is the message of the hero; in fact, one sees him only in the midst of celebrating multitudes.[24]

The mass media are thus the protagonists. The director is the only real disciple who laboriously follows the charismatic leader, the only true believer. Thus the reporter, through the spoken account, is the only witness, but also at the same time the preacher, as one gathers, moreover, from the rapt, ceremonial, or unctuous tone in which the whole scene is described and commented on. In this case the real priest is the commentator; he indeed is entrusted with the synthesis of what the charismatic leader has said, which is never more important, being indeed placed on the same level, than the descriptions of the color, the movements of the crowds, the landscape.

THE MASS MEDIA AND THE ANNULMENT OF DETERMINANTS OF TIME AND PLACE

However, the analysis must be pushed further. To grasp the phenomenological aspects is important, perhaps necessary, but not enough. The TV Pope is probably more the hostage than the beneficiary of the mass media. But it would be ingenuously conspiratorial to consider him an accomplice or consenting victim. It is not just excessive zeal for travel or high-level exhibitionism, but rather an attempt at a reply of the great world religions to the challenge presented by the new synchronic phase we are surely entering. In the course of the past years, alert researchers have provided us with facts and convincing observations on the role, the social placement, and the broad cultural effects of the mass media, without always letting themselves fall into the trap of the indirect defense of the media that hinges on implicit blackmail: now, having admitted that TV causes harm and can extinguish us, if we don't hurry to turn it off, what shall we do? Destroy everything?

Turn back? And what will the babies born in the electronic age do without this dry comforter? And the young mothers, how will they be able to combine career and domestic work without this providential anaesthetic? And what can we say about the camera crews, the thousands and hundreds of thousands of employees, all those who work with the networks, who have with much difficulty acquired very specific technical specializations, knowledge not appplicable in other fields, and a capital of experience that would be lost? Moreover, they hasten to add, these indirect apologists, or hypocrites, appealing to scientific seriousness and rigor, that it is not proved that TV has negative effects, the scenes of violence influence the real behaviour of the young, that its information stays skin-deep and parasitic instead of shaping and educating.

It is true; it is not proven.[25] It is also true that the true heroes of television are really the TV operatives themselves. Their Herculean labors to transmit the images, the technical and environmental difficulties to overcome, the rigors of the climate, always too hot or too cold, the acrobatic attachment of makeshift, dangling wires, given the modest technical level of the environment they find themselves working in for us, only for us, to "bring the world to our home," are meticulously listed. Not only that, but all the names of the participants, the operators, directors, electricians, sound technicians, camera crew, editors, mixers, and so on are duly recorded and credited, before and after the program. Only the year and date of birth are omitted.

And yet all this empirical, detailed literalness is not enough to dispel an overwhelming impression of unreality, as if the camera lens had the strange power not only to photograph but to absorb and dissolve real life, from the "great facts" supposedly historical to the slightest daily behavior, waking, walking, eating, and sleeping in which human beings, "great" and "small" necessarily converge and, at times with some surprise, discover their common humanity. Independently of its specific content, one might say that the television message has the power to create scorched earth, put in brackets and wipe out as irrelevant the "roots" of the human presence on earth. The serials and soap operas, these are instructive: they manage to combine a maximum of escape from reality with a maximum of realism and the everday. They penetrate intimacy, and every viewer finds no difficulty in finding himself there, seeing himself reflected and portrayed with cruel fidelity in certain aspects of life. Yet at the same time these transmissions, which extend episode after episode, infinitely, produce an extreme sense of unreality, of emptiness and squalor, as a contradictory effect. The story that repeats, is equivalent to, itself, with the same emphasized situations, consumes itself, falls victim to a strange law of entropy, annuls itself. It is good for everyone, and so for no one. It loses specificity and hence the character of unique, unrepeatable, and irreducible experience, which truly defines human action and at the same time clarifies its intrinsically unpredictable and dramatic nature.

The TV message is universal, and is adapted to all cultures and countries. The networks are now transnational and can permit themselves the luxury of leaving aside the individual cultures in which they operate not only because the subjects they deal with and which their films abundantly feed off are elementary (mostly sex and violence), but also because they cancel determinants of time and space. Modern technology, on which the mass media are based, has made the venerable old maxim obsolete, "A place for everything and everything in its place." The raw material of the mass media is information; this is very hard material to preserve because, as Goffman noted, it can be stolen without being moved. There is no need to carry it off physically. It is enough to re-transmit it, record it, and repeat it.

The importance of physical presence is seriously threatened. Everything—research, analysis, observation—can be done from a distance. It is rare in the sciences of nature for the scientist to have direct access to natural phenomena. He "reads" the phenomena vicariously by reading the data transmitted by machines. It does not matter where he, physically, personally, is. The wires bring him all the information he needs. It is an antiseptic world, outside time and space. The terminals of the computers give the impression—illusion—of being in touch with the whole world, with tens and thousands of data banks, without leaving home or office. All that can be considered a convenience. So too it was convenient for the armchair sociologists, Durkheim, for example, to study the Australian aborigines without leaving Paris and the warm atmosphere of his own work-room; but nothing can rightly replace presence in the field, direct field research, in daily contact with the human groups being analyzed.

In an age dominated by the mass media and their logic, everything, on the contrary slackens and clouds over. The differences between the sexes tend to be flattened; differences between age-groups disappear; the distinctions between the young and adults are less sharp; adolescence, that modern invention, tends to extend until it is merged in young adults and the adult world. Places and landscapes tend to become the same. The industrial and political managers themselves, the "public men" tend to be flattened as they appear on stage; they lose their mystery and the prestige of distance, that margin of respect (literally *respicere* is "to look at from a certain distance") that once guaranteed their stature, authority, or perhaps more exactly, authoritativeness. At the same time one cannot hastily conclude that thereby the mass media have demystified and stripped power, and constrained it to an immodest striptease. They have simply emptied out the problem of the relation between history and the everyday, power and the masses, by flattening everything; they have made it harder to distinguish, in the undifferentiated quantity of information, what counts and is important from what is less so, or not at all. In this sense they have built a wall of apparent plausibility, made up of pseudo-accounts and pseudo-realism, which scantifies and immortalizes existing social and political conditions.[26]

NOTES

1. This legitimate concern finds at times astonishing expressions. On the authority of Arnaldo Momigliano, who considers biography totally alien to history, a young social historian at the University of Turin, Giovanni Levi, contends that "there must be a reason if for 2000 years history and life histories have been kept apart." It is

striking that this promising scholar would not look for an answer in the elitistic concept of history, traditionally obsessed with the fear of contamination by the supposedly vulgar everyday life.

2. Cf. N. Luhmann, *How Is the Social Order Possible*, Italian translation, Roma-Bari: Laterza, 1985, pp. 131–132 (italics added).

3. See in this connection my *Five Scenarios for the Year 2000*, (Westport: Greenwood, 1986).

4. J. W. Carey, "The Monopoly of Knowledge," in *La Critica Sociologica* 74 (Summer 1985): 14.

5. G. Vattimo, *La Fine Della Modernitá* (Milano: Garzanti, 1985), pp. 15–18.

6. See my article, "L'uomo Nell'era Della Tecnica," in *L'opinione*, May 1985.

7. M. Ciampa, F. Di Stefano, eds., *Sulla Fine Della Storia*, (Naples: Liguori, 1985), p. 132.

8. G. Vattimo, *La Fine Della Modernitá*, pp. 169–170, my emphasis.

9. See on this point my *Trattato di sociologia* (Turin: Utet, 1968), pp. 181 ff.

10. For an authoritative example, see L. Cavalli, *Il capo carismatico* (Bologna: Il Mulino, 1981).

11. See the well-argued, plausible reservations of J. Séguy, "Sociologie générale et sociologie religieuse," in *Archives de Sciences Sociales des Religions* 59, no. 2 (1985): 209.

12. See P. Bourdieu, "Une interprétation de la théorie de la religion selon Max Weber," in *Archives européennes de sociologie* (1971), pp. 3–21. In the *Encyclopedia of the Social Sciences*, E. A. Shils confuses charisma and authority; hence charisma is said to be necessary, in his view, in every political regime and society; as N. Berdyaev would say, the need to "kneel before the prince" thus becomes universal, a characteristic of human nature. Leo Strauss's position is more subtle but equally elitist, wherein the modern political philosopher, the new Plato at the tyrant's court, is said to have the task of educating the "gentleman."

13. Cf. my *Il paradosso del sacro* (Laterza: Rome-Bari, 1983), pp. 127–141. Regarding the People's Temple, I use the as-yet unpublished research of F. Ferrarotti, et al., on the sect of the People's Temple and the mass suicide in Guyana. See especially, for the first Italian analysis of this disturbing phenomenon, where a multidisciplinary study is formulated, my *Inviato speciale al Tempio della morte*, the result of on-the-spot interviews and photographs taken by the

author in San Francisco in the headquarters of the sect, published in the *Corriere della Sera illustrato* 3, no. 9 (3 March 1979): 30–34.

14. Cf. the essays in *Studi sulla produzione sociale del sacro*, (Naples: Liguori, 1978, or the earlier articles by M. I. Macioti and L. Catucci on "Neopentecostali e carismatici," and "I neopentecostali cattolici: dall'irrazionalismo alla salvezza," in *La Critica Sociologica*, no. 43 (Autumn 1977). More recently the subject has been taken up, with special reference to Veneto, by Enzo Pace.

15. Cf. Giancarlo Rocca, *L'Opus Dei. Appunti e documenti per una storia*, ed. Paoline, (Rome: Edizione Paoline, 1985) (moreover, *cum licentia ecclesiastica*); and Klaus Steigleder, *L'Opus Dei vista dall'interno*, Introduction by Maurizio Di Giacomo (Turin: Claudiana, 1986) (Originally published as *Das Opus Dei. Eine Innenansicht*, Köln-Zürich-Einsiedeln: Benziger Verlag, 1983).

16. Cf. Vittorio Lanternari, *Festa, carisma, apocalisse* (Palermo: Sellerio, 1983). Recently a report was published, edited by the Segretariato per l'Unione dei Cristiani, del Segretariato per i non Cristiani, del Segretariato per i non Credenti e del Pontificio Consiglio per la Cultura, a "provisional report based on (about 75) replies and documents received 30 October 1980 from the regional and national episcopal conferences." It was published under the title, *Il fenomeno delle sette o nuovi movimenti religiosi. Sfida pastorale*.

17. Giorgio Bartolomei, Crescenzo Fiore, *I nuovi monaci, Hare Krsna: ideologia e pratica di un movimento neo-orientale* (Milan: Feltrinelli, 1981). While the study leaves in obscurity the data regarding the life preceding contact with and joining the Hare Krishna group, It is a useful source for the description of daily life within the movement and the processes of socialization and learning. As regards Transcendental Meditation, cf. M. I. Macioti, *Teoria e tecnica della pace interiore. Saggio sulla Meditazione Trascendentale* (Naples: Liguori, 1980).

18. ASUMC, *I principi. Un'esposizione. Lo livello* 1983 (Universal Principles of the SAUCW). The quotations used here are taken from this. For another version of Moon's theory, cf. *Unification Thought through Study Guide*, (New York: Unification Thought Institute, 1974).

19. Sun Myung Moon, *La famiglia: fonte di felicità* (from the address *The True Pattern of Family Life*, given by Moon to ASUMC/SAUCW members), nn.195-6, (July-August 1985): 8.

20. *Today's World*, July 1982: on the cover there is a picture of the event and the ceremony (held on June 20 of the same year) of a wedding celebrated for more than 2000 couples: the spouses need not necessarily know each other beforehand. The Holy Wedding of 2075

82   The End of Conversation

couples was enlivened by the presence of True Parents, whose black and white photo takes up a full page.

21. On the "image of power and power of the image," see the research I coordinated for the RAI's office of program research, published in 1985. A specific study on the Pope's image in relation to the mass media was announced by G. Guizzardi in *CISR, Actes 18ème Conférence Internationale* (Louvain: 1985), pp. 24–35.

22. P. Apolito, "Il popolo del papa," *La critica sociologica* 77 (Spring 1986), in which the papal visit to Salerno is reported and commented upon.

23. Cf. the research coordinated by G. Guizzardi, *CISR, Actes 18ème Conferénce*, p. 27.

24. *Ibid*, p. 28.

25. Even in Italy the material on this is endless. See especially the works by C. Bechelloni, G. Gamaleri, F. De Domenico, S. Livolsi, for an overview; though personal and rather selective, see R. Grandi, *Comunicazioni di massa* (Bologna: Clueb, 1984).

26. For a typical example of the ambivalence with which these subjects are treated even by particularly intelligent analysts, see J. Meyrowitz, *No Sense of Place* (New York: Oxford University Press, 1985).

3

New Historicism and Life Histories

THE CRISIS OF HISTORICISM

The crisis and limitations of historicism are embodied acutely and persuasively by Max Weber. Herein lies his importance. He stood firmly at the intersection between petrified paleo-positivism and cloudily internalizing idealism. I am not refer-ring to his methodological studies, but to the foundation of his sociology. He intended it to be "understanding" (*vcrotchonla*) but at the same time it aspired to understand what had not yet been heard or listened to. Clearly nothing instructive could come to this sociology from outside and from below: that is, from the common people living day by day in the framework of an everyday existence by definition assumed to be grey and without "noble values." Weber's sociology was based on the idea of the historical individual, following an original outline and a series of proposals, both theoretical and political, which he derived primarily from Heinrich Rickert and Emil Lask, but which seem unable to resist the attack of the pure epis-temologists. The supreme value one can logically derive from it is that of the *Kulturmensch*, or man in the complete sense, able to make conscious choices between alternative values. But the irrational gap between concept and reality was not bridged.

On the contrary, his solution presupposed such dualism, and it is fair to say that Weber did not manage to grasp Rickert's basic arguments. These, however, were vital for his theoretical model, and in this way he became the prisoner of a non sequitur from which he could find only a pragmatic way out by evoking the double ethical responsibility of principles and decision. The pure epistemologists could thus conclude that his sociology was impossible, could not exist, and if it did, should not have done.

The risk of this reduction *ad absurdum* is that Weber ended up by criticizing his own essential, most important, contribution: the open system, the notion of a methodology created in the living process of research instead of being coldly presumed in the study, on the basis of preconstituted categories. Weber's probably insurmountable limitation should not be sought there.[1] It concerned the concept of history which was still elitist and restricted, limited to the peaks of society and the exclusive prerogatives of their power. This conception is no longer sufficient. Even in Weber's time it could not account for the upsurge of the ineffable and mysterious, perhaps omnipotent, grace of the charismatic leader. However, history is not a river, relatively unilinear, nor yet a flood. Rather, it is a delta with many outlets, discharging from shifting contours, and covered with Cimmerian clouds, to the extend that no one has been able to describe its complex outspreading accurately. One can understand the simplifying concern of the traditional historians, who prefer to tread the relatively well-beaten and squared-off paths of *histoire-bataille* rather than the twisting tracks of *histoire-homme*. Their philological care deserves full appreciation, but their perspective needs broadening quite basically. Witnesses must be added to the documents and monuments. Oral testimonies, alive, steeped in the warmth of the present and the living, alarming, upsetting factors of the orderly flow of historical events. And yet, it is not just today that: "torrentiality was not a fantastic accident which arrived to disturb history, and then to be re-absorbed. Rather, it was the manifestation of the new dominant character . . . joined on to history, transforming it for ever after."[2]

This complicated history escapes the traditional categories, convenient perhaps, but narrow. The entrenched disciplinarians were shaken by it. Political history, or at most intellectual history, that is, the history of the summit, was forced to broaden its perspectives, become social history and history of institutions, of custom, of average behavior, of economics, and of *mentalités*. From being historical history, more or less granitic, it melted into the problematic fluidity of life histories. The history of princes had to welcome—and accept being rewritten as—a history of subjects. The historical and the experienced began to give way to a subtle, unexplored dialectic of relationships. It has been penetratingly observed:

Human history is the locus of mediation. It is not only knowledge bound to a perimeter of a discipline, but the experience of memories and facts, the sense of belonging to situations, processes, and results. To cut off the mediating action from specific contexts by taking possession of it as a value complete in itself, means removing it from the richness and testing of the chance interweavings of the experienced.[3]

It is hereby made clear that the break between history and the everyday is problematic. As soon as we ask, "Who makes history?" this gap becomes insupportable. Just as, on the other hand, understanding without first listening is a clear contradiction, an obvious absurdity. It can only be explained by forgetting that for the *Kulturmensch* there is nothing (outside his own interiority and that of the few like him) to listen to, because there is nothing in the plebeians or human masses really meaningful worth listening to. It also thereby makes clear why the everyday is believed to be banal, opaque, and lacking incognitive value. This was clearly the price owed to the myth of the great individual. In this context, culture appears as a knowledge with an authoritarian structure, in the face of a latent Ego that has stayed infantile. It is symptomatic that authors are quoted only by observing them from without. There is quotation and re-quotation. It is a culture which rises before the Ego like a wall to be scaled, a commodity to be possessed, grasped, a prison wall: a culture in which one does not participate. Either one dominates or is dominated. There is no active contemplation, calm acceptance, or tranquil agreement to be achieved thought by thought, permitted to exist on its own terms. Rather, this culture is presented as an activistic task, an end to strive towards, summed up in affirmation, in thinking how to compete, prevaricate, and command. Experience of the Ego as experience of the ordinary is excluded on principle. In this sense, it is still an authoritarian and elitist culture. It is the culture of history as a phenomenon simply of the summit; from Cicero to the mass media, a *paideia* or *Bildung*, hinging on the ideas of the gentleman in Leo Strauss or Plato.

And yet, history is nothing other than the sedimentation of the lived, tracing the footsteps of whoever passed by first, examining the tracks of whoever already crossed or is crossing, deciphering and connecting them. In this sense history is both time and space: rootedness. For centuries, change has been insisted on as a factor in, or more simply the occasion for, emancipation. One tends to equate mobility and freedom. In the *Manifesto*, Marx and Engels exalt the revolutionary role of the capitalist bourgeoisie that swept away the "idiocies of rural life." If human beings need change and innovation, they also, however, need stability and security. The most incorrigible nomad is such in relation to an *ubi consistam*, his landscape of the soul. He, too, perhaps especially, needs roots. Petty, short-term politics has ruined many ancient, venerable expressions. Among them is "living space," *Lebensraum*. Human beings do not live in the void. They need a territory to root themselves in. They create their horizon, a familiar landscape, on time for the appointment every morning, human space. This is not a concession to the grossest ethology, still less to the hasty equation between human and animal worlds. The human animal does not have the rigidities of behavior, not yet the enviable instrumental endowments, of his brothers. He does not go on heat in certain, unchanging months of the year. He does not just have instinct. Hence there is nothing monodic in him, nothing completely pre-established or programmed. The sense of belonging has the same variability as a melody the capricious, unpredictable wind brings near and wafts away. He knows moments of exceptional intensity wherein many places are concentrated and harmonized existentially in the psychic memory of the individual; the phases of relative tiredness. I clearly remember the tower of Champ du Feu, the quiet, perfumed green of the sanctuary of St. Odile in Alsace. Ancient mountains, the Vosges, engraved with history and the tart scent of homemade wine, camels bent, night-marching, like the well-loved mountains of Sabina I gaze at in the moonlight on August nights at Terminillo, like the breached hills of my native Monferrato, green and burnt at the same time, over by Camino, Tagliaferro, Ozzano, Fabiano, and Brusaschetto. The ordinary in reality is extraordinary: to be convinced of this it suffices to look at it long enough, with the necessary calm to penetrate its deceptive surfaces, the protective film that insidiously enfolds this place of secrets.[4]

So, history and the everyday. The history of historicism is exhausted. It has reached the terminus. I do not intend using the term "historicism" in the way E. H. Carr rebuked Popper for using it: "Professor Popper uses the term 'historicism' as an epithet, good for all purposes, for every opinion on history he does not approve of."[5] However, it seems generally agreed that a history is commencing, so diverse that to some it has appeared as a post-history. What does it mean? Is it possible to live without history? The common people have often enjoyed the favors of the powerful as the captivating puppy wins the distracted caress of the passing guest. That is no longer enough. The puppies have grown. Knowledge can no longer pose as a private capital, privately accumulated, as a presupposition for the power structure. It is, all in all, a fragile construct. True: the great ideas, extraordinary events, the dates that make history have been duly recorded. But these are only the explosions, unexpected and noisy, of long, obscure, and mysterious tensions. These must be explored in their slow, magmatic formation. A human footprint on the sand. It is a sign, but also a symbol. A human being has passed by. He has left a track. Where was he going? Where did he come from? His passing has a meaning. Sign, symbol, meaning. Finally—word.

HISTORY AND SOCIOLOGY

The relation between history and sociology must be taken away from immediate polemics and re-worked as a function of research. The witty remarks of a scholar such as Paul Veyne, among others, are no longer enough.[6] His brilliant anti-sociological polemic on Italian culture is now old and traditionalized, both in the spiritualistic version and the neo-idealist one; it even has its classics from Benedetto Croce to Ugo Spirito, by way of Monsignor Olgiati. It is a delaying polemic, so concerned with finding the right word that it seems a cross between a fencing bout and a kind of intellectual ballet. It is a real pity that the dance, in itself enjoyable, should rest everything on a conception of science which has had its day. As Eugenio Garin, in this case a source above suspicion, would say, this is a conception typical of the "less sagacious positivists."[7] Reductive and crude, which presumes to be able to ask contemporary sciences their particulars (definition, object, methods) like a zealous, plodding policeman asking the passers-by for their documents. As, for example, he does not manage *a priori* to identify the object of sociology, the author concludes it does not exist, as "every science has its object" (p. 460).

A little earlier, history was liquidated, as it is either total history or nothing. Total history is not possible, at least for the moment; one would have to pass from history linked to major events to that concerned with the everyday. In other words, one would have to pass from dynastic history, that of the summit, to economic history, social history, or history in dialogue with sociology. Yet Veyne has scarcely finished showing, in his view, that sociology understands nothing, only to add in the grip of a sudden repentence, that history can exist and have meaning only on condition it ingests sociology. The *jeu de massacre* is lively and written well, even entertainingly, but restricts itself to destroying and hitting ready-made targets. It recalls certain Papini-esque swipes. To go down well, Veyne's game would need pepper and salt if the sciences were really those strict enclosures the bright French historian imagines: lightly confusing reasons for the organizational subdivision of scientific work and teaching (knowing, for example, who should examine whom and on what), with basic questions, and grasping nothing of the multidisciplinary approach. However, at the level of critical discussion all this is water under the bridge. The surprise, or rather the scandal, exists only for the half-informed, dabblers or learned as they may be. Croce, from whom Veyne borrows regarding the origin of sociology, ever with Durkheim as target (see p. 460 ff; for Croce, see the review of an article by Durkheim in *La Critica*, vol. 1, pp. 55–56), was much subtler, even though ignorant of scientific procedure which, moreover, he tagged contemptuously as mere hypotheticism.

Veyne's brilliant work thus runs the risk of being reduced to a lawyer's tirade. His powder is rather damp. Whoever today could imagine defining any science in the abstract? Wherever could one find an inventor with such a straightjacket? For what hidden mystery of obtuseness could he not perceive that defining a science *a priori* means taking as already obtained the results of research not even begun? Whoever believes today it possible to determine the sciences on the basis of their own conceptual categorizations, or a personal effort unconnected with operational research, is a pathetic character who thinks about and concerns himself with today's problems with, to say the least, nineteenth-century criteria. In contemporary conditions of scientific work one can say that a science exists when a certain manner of reasoning and orienting research on given themes has been crystallized. The attempt, instead, to define from the outside either science in general or specific sciences not only implies the rather crude notion of a reality to be investigated, congealed and closed on itself. This must be supposed to lend itself to be nicely divided into as many segments or game reserves as there are sciences named as legitimate and as have aspirations to become involved with them. It also stands as the exemplary expression of a mechanistic attitude that confuses science with scientism. We have arrived at Comtean imperialism turned upside down, a real boomerang.

Going into details, some clarifications are needed. From the earliest pages in which Veyne deals with Weber, he relegates him to the motley legion of the disciples of Friedrich

Nietzsche—certainly not a contemptible company, but far from doing justice to the quite specific torments of the Erfurt sociologist. Veyne must have scented in the heroic stoicism (at least, Calvinistic stoicism) of Weber's "polytheism of values" and the existential stress that formed and surrounded it, ample traces of a romantic superman kind. I can understand the haste of a champion of "broadened history" (p. 43 ff.) But here he tends to exaggerate. It is easier when one is content to break down unlocked doors. That history is ideographic, that is, concerns itself with the specific, or that the facts "have no absolute rank," that is, do not speak for themselves, as even the most modest researcher knows very well, is self-evident. However, in general the polemic approach of Veyne is confined to seizing what is already known. History as reconstruction of interconnections is a good idea, but, with the derided notion of relation to values, was already exposed by Weber: That there are no jumps between nature and history, as the great names of German historicism (Rickert, Dilthey) theorized on the other hand, was a need that the most aware sociologists have long faced by filling the gap on the one hand between sciences of nature and on the other of the social sciences, or sciences of culture, as Weber like to say—without, however, making summary identifications for pure love of paradox.

One might say regarding Weber, as of sociology in general, that Veyne always follows the same tactical rule: to attack to the limit that one paraphrases. Naturally, the relations between history and sociology are a serious matter. Strict positivists and more or less absolute historicists have done their best to disparage the two disciplines to one another. This claim did not wait for Paul Veyne's *bons mots* and is essentially the product of a misunderstanding that implies a conception of sociological analysis of a still Comtean kind, systematic in an all-embracing, closed sense. On the other hand, it implies historical research that strives to coincide with all humankind and all our possible creations. But to deny the possibility of a reduction or mechanistic synthesis of the two disciplines does not mean ignoring their necessary collaboration and the essentially complementary aspects uniting them. The problem is different; it should be expressed rigorously by posing an explicit question: what sociology can open itself positively to collaboration with history, and on the other hand, what history can expect good results from a collaboration with sociology?

For a response on the criticial level to this question, it would be as well to briefly consider the evolution of relations between history and sociology.[8] A first phase seems marked by the clear differentiation which rests on the conception of historical narration as individualizing narration, and of sociological analysis as study tending towards generalization. The relation thus seems to be reduced to the polarity between idiographic and nomothetic moments, and between the conception of historical development as diachronic process, uni- or plurilinear, and as synchronic process, with a multiplicity of interdependent variables. From this viewpoint, the contradiction between history and sociology appears simply irremediable. There probably derives from this the tendency and temptation of a summary reduction of the two disciplines one to another. However, not only is this claim unjustifiable, as it is still based on an a critical notion both of history and sociology, but also because within narrative history itself a highly interesting development has been taking place. The perspective of the austere political history of Thucydides has been broadening out to the point where the question of the tension between particular and general, and thus between idiography and the nomothetic, is not only marked in that between history and sociology. It is also emerging within the historical discourse, and, as Bruno Gentili remarked, it is expressed in the dialectical relation between sources and interpretation. I should humbly add, in the idea of the general context in which the historical discourse necessarily takes place.

Here we arrive at the second stage of the history-sociology relationship. The historians are beginning to use sociological categories capable of bringing together in a single meaningful context a complex of information and empirical data (for example, think of Arnold Toynbee's schema "challenge" and "response" as a celebrated example). Leaving aside for now, and here, the consideration of how much lack of critical quality there still is in the surreptitious use of sociological categories that are not clearly expounded, I am driven to remark how the historical discourse is worthily being freed from its purely individual,[9] creative-artistic progression. It is instead seeking to provide itself with instruments capable of grasping not only (and not so much) the diachronic sequence as summed up in the fate and attitudes of the peaks or summits of society, to the point of being reduced to political, or at most intellectual history. Rather, it is striving to grasp also the synchronic perspective: otherwise, it is broadening out towards a conception of historical experience as social experience, economic and cultural in the broad sense. Those worlds judged alien to the dynastic and elitist argument are shown to be important, not only as collateral and additional indicators, but as indispensable spies for the understanding of the quality of a specific historical life. The everyday environmental conditions, social relations at the local level, fashion, cuisine, economic forces and their relations, the state of development of techniques and their impact on the life of communities, and so on—these are the spies. This is the methodological sense, not a grossly value-laden one, of the formula "history from below." That this approach should then have major, serious consequences of an interpretative kind should not deter us from considering its contribution in purely cognitive terms.

This point still seems to escape many analysts and serious scholars, among them G. Cotrone.[10] Concerned with defending even the letter of Croce's teaching, he does not grasp its limits. These are linked with a conservative choice of unusual coherence, which sees in the masses nothing more than an inert fuel, and in their attempts at rising up little more than a curio, retaining for the summits of society, along with economic and social privileges, the prerogative of scientific knowledge and moral wisdom. On the contrary, Oscar Lewis's and Studs Terkel's research, along with that of Danilo Montaldi, Pietro Crespi, and Nuto Revelli, is exemplary, but not to be read if prospecting for folkloristic curiosities or presumed gems of popular culture. Croce was right when he wrote in an autobiographic vein:

Even we critics and historians of literature have been forced to abandon the dear, gentle myth of popular poetry, the fresh, original voice
of the people, which is supposed from time to time to dissolve the
aged, dried-out artistic poetry and give life to new forms and new
works of genius.[11]

In other words, it is not a matter of mythologizing an *anti-
quissima Italorum sapientia*. Nor is it one of seizing from the
so-called popular culture the elements of a undefined, misty,
and conceptually elusive culture of contestation. What seems
important is the accurate recording and understanding of the
subordinate viewpoint as regards its content of cognitive validity. Thus there should be no indulgence towards demagogic
Third Worldiness, but rather a widening of the traditional
historical perspective through the use of new instruments: a
critical use presented as a crucial movement towards the set-
ting-up of a neo-historicism beyond the limits of classical historicism. In this light the contribution of life-histories as an
analytical and interpretative instrument can be decisive.

LIFE-HISTORIES AND THE HISTORICAL
HORIZON

The critical demands made of the proposal in my *History
and Life-Histories*[12] are relevant here. According to Italo
Mancini, I am victim in this book of a serious logical contradiction.[13] In his view: "It is entrusted to 'life-histories' to set
up a social and historical horizon, and then this is postulated
so that life-histories do not fall into 'psychism' and appear as
social phenomena." A little earlier in the same article Mancini stressed the "tiresome dilemma" in which Dilthey's reflection on the "space of identity between life produced and
life understood" found itself, so to speak, ensnared. Mancini
thinks he perceives a similar difficulty in my work where I
suggest a clear and radical conflict with both paleo-positivist
quantification and vague, mystifying psychologism, an orientation of sociological research based on the methodology of lis-

tening. I fear my proposal is more complex than Mancini believes, and escapes the narrows of binary reasoning.

What seems to Mancini a tiresome contradiction—and in
fact, apart from the tiresomeness, there are no contradictions
that do not challenge or at least to some extent weaken an
argument—is but the reflection of the very difficult, polydi-
mensional nature of these problems. There are also apparent
contradictions and necessary contradictions when the themes
covered touch on several conceptual planes, and have such
complexity as to challenge and make their reduction to formal
abstraction logically impossible, without leading to their flattening out into reductionist, schematic one-sidedness. I am sorry
for the somewhat heavy-handed way of describing it, but this
operation is more common than normally believed and basically lies in making the complexity of problems suffer for the
conceptual and technical inadequacy of the orientation of the
study.

In Mancini's view, the contradiction principally concerns the
notion of "historical horizon." I admit to making use here of a
convenient short-hand phrase. First, this expression means the
non-intemporal character of auto-biographical documents; that
of *not* being unrooted from extra-subjective material determi-
nations. However, secondly, it also indicates a term which,
though external, is not thereby transcendant as regards life-
histories. It is made up of the totality of structural relations
in the extra-subjective sense, endowed with their materiality,
close to Durkheim's "thing-ness," be it solidified into formally
codified institutions or, rather, embodied into behavior and
custom. What escapes Mancini is the relation necessarily established between the two terms, the historical horizon and
life-histories, understood as the plane of experience. Between
these poles there appears a field of mediations still to be explored, and which on the other hand neither Dilthey's solution, which is still psychologizing, nor dogmatic Marxism (or
dialecticized, in the canonical form of Stalinist Diamat) is able
to pose at the critical level.

I think that only by neglecting this theoretical limit can
Mancini reasonably attribute to me the unexpectedly polemical intention of "putting the Marxist theory of society in cri-

sis." As regards Dilthey, the psychologistic limitation seems clear, as even a hasty reading of the *Critique of Historical Reason* could easily demonstrate, and as one sees in the author's very words:

> The *Erlebnis* is real as a *fact of consciousness*, and so too every part contained in it. And every representation indicates something real, if it takes place directly. Thus the reality of the particular *Erlebnis* is here elevated to *objectively valid knowledge* in the concepts, judgments and psychological connections.[14]

Givenness is thus reabsorbed and subsumed in a pure internal connection of an essential psychic nature, whose morphological and phenomenological analysis is legitimately demanded by Dilthey from descriptive psychology. In Marx, on the other hand, givenness is basic. The theoretico-conceptual apparatus is weighty vis-à-vis the dynamics of the historical formation of capitalism as system set in motion by an impersonal logic. It explains in large measure the lasting validity of the Marxian theory of society as a global reality in movement. The missing pole is the experienced. The dialectical relation between givenness and the experienced comes out defective: it turns about itself, impoverished in a short circuit that diminishes its range and internal richness. The actors in the historic process are faceless, and run the risk of the interchangeable anonymity of the mannequin. The circumscribed base of human experience is clouded. The dialectical process is flattenend out into an abstract, mystified dialectic, ready to serve as summary justification for bureaucratized practice.

My proposal not only is not intended to bring fuel to the fires of fashionable anti-Marxism, but strives—something that could also be regarded as presumption—to rediscover the deep purpose of the Marxian theory of society. It is not a matter of mechanically hanging up the tatters of dated, lived human experience—life-histories, supposedly—on a hypothetical "historical horizon," but rather to grasp the connection of reciprocal conditioning running between the different levels of experience and between these and the structural, macro-systemic level. In this way one fixes the prime elements of a *re-*

lational dialectic wherein nature and culture, environment and history, system, class, group, and individual enter into a relationship among themselves that is both necessary and *a priori* (dogmatically), not precisely and quantitatively predictable. From the strictly operational-methodological viewpoint, I am suggesting the examination of the events of situation (decision, fact, history at the macro-social systematic level) as it appears at the systemic, structural level according to a triple grid that explains, describes, and interprets the intersection with the sub-systemic community (how it is perceived, known, evaluated, and reacted to at the local level.

The analysis must also discuss the intersection with the level of the experience of the primary group and of the individual as socialized and thus instituted as a person in the group. No doubt this involves a new conception of historicity. This is a post-historicist historicity, not so much concerned with the capital or small letter of history as with recognizing and conceptually doing justice to the complexity of the social. This last is ever more synchronic, interdependent, rich with new potential but at the same time elusive and hard to decipher by using categories that are perhaps also familiar and testing but pre-constituted and certainly today inadequate.

PRELIMINARY CRITICAL REMARKS

In the general plan of my work, life-histories are thus a crucial instrument on the way to the new critical historicism, following the false exits from the crisis of classical historicism that are now being attempted. Here I limit myself to discussing:

A. Systems theory

B. Structural-functionalism in its weak form (Parsons, Merton), and its strong variation (Luhmann)

C. Scientistic structuralism, as with Althusser, who ends up by dehistoricizing Marxism in the fashion of the vetero- and neo-Stalinist dogmatists of Diamat

D. Socio-biology, or belated Spencerism

E. Ethno-methodology and symbolic interactionism, with the implicit psychologizing of the social

F. The psychoanalytic attitude as total explanation, with its elementary nostalgic impulses

G. Irrational decisionism (Carl Schmitt), and

H. Structural semiology, which views society as nothing more than a linguistic metaphor.

The crisis of historicism is a real one, but is not a prelude to the end of history. It serves rather to indicate the end of historical development as a diachronic movement, seeing in Western European civilization its basic inspiration and ultimate goal. The synchrony of the new "choral" and group-centered age involves the exhaustion of elitist and dynastic historicism, which one leaves by way of the broadening of perspective, on the basis of the concept of history as historical life in the full sense, polysemic and polymorphous.

The objections raised against the biographical method, which might be more precisely described as the biographical approach (such is the variety of the paths and so multiple the basis of the arguments it permits and indeed demands), are well-known. The champions of traditional quantitative methods, with worthy diligence never tire of recalling them. They speak of the biographical method as of a passing fashion, which they do not hesitate to present as the portent of grave damage, whose seriousness, however, ill fits the ultimately fragile and friable nature of the fashion so denounced. One or the other: either the fashion is really such, and it would not be worthwhile worrying about its fleeting capriciousness, or the damage it causes is really serious, and then we are not dealing with fashion but errors of great import. The latter alternative would seem the more plausible, bearing in mind that the damage feared, aside from methodological infatuation, concerns the de-professionalization of sociological work, the rejection of analysis as a distancing from the path of scientific work, and an inevitable sinking in the swamp of irresponsible subjectivism.

These fears are not wholly groundless. They must on the

contrary be expressed in their real terms and requisite implications. There is no doubt that the biographical method, as
we shall see, ends the separation, the real disparity of power,
that today occurs between researcher and object of research.
The objectualization of human groups to be analysed is incompatible with the biographical method and its scientific outlook. Between researcher and object there is not only a process of interaction. The critical character of research also
demands, first of all, that one recognize how each researcher
in the human sciences is also researched, without which one
falls into the naturalistic reification of the object, worthy of
the worst paleo-positivism.

This does not mean at all transforming scientific research
into a kind of thought fair. It simply means not smuggling in
any detective's report as sociological research. Sociology is not
sociography, and still less mineralogy. One understands the
concern of sociological professionalism. Indeed, any service activity, performed for money on behalf of a customer who has
no possibility of checking the service itself, is called a profession. In this sense, sociological research does not enter into
the picture of current professionalism. Only someone who believes they are in a market, ready to sell themselves to the
highest bidder, independently of his particular problematic but,
rather, disposed to research any subject or problem so long as
he finds a client ready to pay and cover expenses, can feed a
conception which reduces sociology to a collection of applied
techniques, ideally indifferent and netural, and thereby basically interchangeable.

No one intends, furthermore, to compete with James Joyce's
stream of consciousness, nor wishes to emulate the model of
the open-ended work. However, that scientific discourse is
typically closed has yet to be shown, aside from the far from
unlikely risk that in this way one may fall into a rabbinical
or priestly conception of the scientist, placed above social interests and the struggle between groups and classes, a disembodied angel fluttering above the weaknesses of common mortals and their history made up of plots, power struggles,
violence, and blood, rather than of scientific records accurately transcribed. In what sense can we speak of a closure of

the scientific method? Does it mean we must arrive at assertions which tend in the last resort towards the universally meaningful? But then there is the danger of a closure that impoverishes the discourse and research through the extreme of tautology or statement of the obvious. Or else that closure is inevitable in any scientific argument that rejects the inductive method and only uses the deductive method? But then must we really abandon Francis Bacon to return to Aristotle?

What can be disturbing in the objections made to the biographical method is the tendency to wish to judge it not in its own terms but rather by turning to the evaluative criteria of metrical inference, as though to know scientifically was of necessity the same as measuring quantitatively, with no residues, and as though the clinical approach and statistical representatives were the same thing. This procedure seems to me at once illegitimate, unwarranted, and misleading. It makes itself an easy target, which it calls the biographical method, and then claims to destroy it with conceptual instruments and criteria that have nothing in common with it. It is, however, useful to attempt a reply however preliminary, to be taken up again and developed elsewhere, to the more common objections which have generally circulated among the more zealous champions of quantitative methods.

I shall try to summarise the most important aspects of this critical apparatus:

1. The researcher must limit himself to the clear and reproducible presentation of inferences.

2. One must ask what is the condition whereby an individual history refers back to the social. If *one* biography is enough to read a society, any biography must be that one. But then do all individual histories, in their absolutely unique subjectivity, constitute the re-appropriation of the same social? All equally?

3. There is biographical material more illuminating than others; there is biographical material which does not, at an appreciably observable level, summarize certain aspects of society. The hypothesis of reading a society through *one* biography, *one* specific, summarizing practice cannot be sustained.

One must at once stress that it is not by chance that after having mentioned the theme of representivity, one mostly finds the theme that appears decisive: that of inference. The question of inference is seen as a function of the understanding of the level of saturation of variability, which is the impression of not having anything more to learn. If inference is really a function of saturation, then we have enough elements to understand what is the intimate logic of the followers of quantitative methods: the logic of snath and grab, abandonment of the inverted logic of the Ogino-Knaus method (one must hope to question the social in its fertile periods).

The most important points of the argument are:

4. Are there different kinds of scientific inference? That is, are there inferences constructed and repeatable (hence checkable) on the basis of considerations of a metric kind and inferences which, on the contrary, produce complete abstraction, as regards logical methods of identification, formulation, and control by metrical considerations? In other words, is there a possibility of an inference absolutely independent of the concept (and operation) of measurement, even understanding the latter in the broadest, most comprehensive sense?

5. Other objections then involve the inductive method and the non-divisability of problems of inference and replicability: that is, how to identify the reasons allowing one to believe true a given assertion and the reasons permitting one to continue to believe it true (after a certain lapse of time).

6. Objections are extended finally to the hypothesis of the construction of the analysis through the whole process of research (this hypothesis criticizes the method of analysis as *a posteriori* analysis to the gathering of data, as final demiurgic act): returning once more to the nub of inference, it has been argued that as the final inference is also an objective of biographical method, there are no differences between the biographic and the neo-positivist method (the study of the saturated whole as common denominator of the two approaches).

These critical remarks tend to identify in the inductive method and subjectivism the mark of a weak epistemological basis to the biographical method. The premise of such a sociological study is in fact the preliminary decision of what it is intended to research: it is argued that the particular tells us something only when we already know the general universe to which it refers. Outside such reference the particular is either unknown or appears irrelevant. Thus strictly speaking, the biographical method needs to be referred to deduction, not induction. But if we read biography with the deductive procedure, we implicitly strip the biographical method of any epistemological significance. Whether we refer to the inductive or to the deductive method, the biographical one has no hope.

Now let us try to draw together the threads of all these arguments, developing the criticisms point by point, and trying finally to organize them into a coherent whole.

INFERENCE AND REPRODUCIBILITY

One criticism levelled against the biographical method concerns the problems of inference and reproducibility of these inferences. It is correct to postulate the essential unity of the two moments, but not sufficient. One has to make explicit the original contents and concepts that structure the two problems. It is equally necessary to determine the nature of the relation which binds the two problems. In relation to that, one should point out how in current methodology inference is a function of its reproducibility; that, is, it is so constructed. Thus the concept of reproducibility and models of it become important. As regards models, one can think either of a logico-semantic model (where the central element is the transparency and formal clarity of the categories, concepts, and words used), or a logico-historical one (where the re-impact with the reality studied is central). It seems to me that the problem of reproducibility always required a model of the second type. If this approach is acceptable, there are two concepts which are rarely explained. The first is that of continuity, which expresses a kind of diachronic uniformity (an atemporal prolongation of synchronic uniformity): the other is that of repeatability (as against that of uniqueness or singularity).

As Karl Popper does, it is correct in scientific work to distinguish between "happening" and "event' and add as a third element "process." In Popper, the happening is what is described by a singular statement, the event is "what is typical, or universal, in a happening." (*The Logic of Scientific Discovery*, pp. 78–80). A process is a group of happenings and events perceived in their flux. The uniqueness of the happening and the typicalness of the event are the basic ingredients of scientific research: they are precious goods the researcher must handle with care, by establishing—flexibly—the procedures of finding and the procedures of justifying (H. Reichenbach). The process is, on the other hand, metaphorically the sea in which one may sink or float. This risk is present in all scientific work, leaving aside the method or methods employed and their strength: scientific work is a human undertaking.

The hypothesis of reproducibility requires of the researcher and his apparatus the ability to decipher the repeatability of a phenomenon. Popper is again of help in focussing on this aspect:

The basic doctrine, which runs beneath all theories of induction, is the *doctrine of the primacy of repetitions*. Bearing in mind the attitude of Hume, we can distinguish two variants of this doctrine. The first (criticized by Hume) can be called the doctrine of the logical primacy of repetitions. According to this doctrine, the repetition of cases provides a kind of *justification* for the acceptance of a universal law. (The idea of repetition is usually linked to that of probability). The second (which Hume supported) may be called the doctrine of temporal (and psychological) primacy of repetitions. By this second doctrine, repetitions, even if they do not manage to provide any kind of *justification* for a universal law and the expectations and beliefs that entails, in fact they induce and arouse in us these expectations and beliefs, however little this fact (or belief) may be "justified" or "rational" (p. 475).

For Popper, both doctrines are unsustainable.

Popper stresses that repetitions are approximate (phenomena are similar in their repetitions). Now, in similarity of two phenomena (the second of which is a repetition of the first) always presupposes the

adoption of a point of view: some similarities or repetitions strike us if a certain problem interests us. But if the similarity and the repetition presuppose the adoption of a point of view, or an interest or expectation, it is logically necessary that the points of view, interests or expectations be logically and temporally (or by chance or psychologically) first, as regards repetition. But this result destroys both the doctrine of the logical primacy and that of the temporal primacy of repetitions (pp. 476–477).

Popper's conclusion is still clearer:

We can add the remark that given any group or finite whole of things, however variously we have selected them, we can always with a little ingenuity find points of view such that all the things belonging to that whole, considered from one of these points of view, are similar (or partially equal): this means that one may say anything of a repetition of any thing. This shows how ingenuous it is to consider repetition as something definitive or given (p. 477).

Clearly, there is rigor and rigor. If we move on from Popper to H. Blalock, we note a profound difference of style, due perhaps to what is for me the basic difference between American and European culture: the abundance in European culture of philosophical knowledge, the search for the "deep breath."
Blalock writes:

By common consent, reality, or at least our perception of reality, lies in on-going processes. Two events never repeat themselves exactly, nor does any object or organism stay the same from one minute to another. And yet, if we want to understand the nature of the real world, we have to act and think as if events repeated themselves and as if objects really had certain properties which stay constant during a certain period of time, however short. If we prevent ourselves from assuming these simple hypotheses, we shall never be able to make generalizations which go beyond the individual event (*L'analisi causale in sociologia*, p. 90).

Returning to our initial problem (inference as function of replicability), it should be stressed here how replicability within a logico-historical model is possible when the phenomena studied are typical, uniform, and repeatable (in the sense that when we replicate them there is no risk of finding ourselves faced with something completely different, or that we shall not find it again). However, and this is the crucial point, to what extent is a process of totality of uniform and repeatable events, that is, in a state of equilibrium (even if dynamic)? Again, are all phenomena repeatable? And do all manifest themselves in a continuous manner? Do those disturbances Blalock speaks of (p. 262) depend on "variables left out of the theoretical system" or, rather on the interference of causes which act discontinuously and end up complicating the model when we least expect it?

What we find, then, is an arguable (and perhaps illegitimate) use of the concept of equilibrium. This concept is no longer related to the synchronic level (by studying, for example, the relations between the parts of a system or between occurrences separated by a very short space of time), but is extended to the diachronic plane, if only surreptitiously. When, for example, it is argued that a given historico-social situation arises, comes from a preceding situation, in a more or less linear manner, one is reasoning in terms of equilibrium, of linear links that should not be assumed as problems to explain but rather as expressions of the internal, natural logic, proper to almost all social facts. Every fact has its antecedent which justifies and explains it. The concept of equilibrium applied at the diachronic level performs the function of providing historico-social occurrences with an evolutionary logic, which to be both logical and evolutionary, cannot admit the existence of leaps, voids, unexpected eruptions, differences so small as to be imperceptible. It does not admit dis-connections.

The idea of equilibrium and continuity in social facts thus seems at the basis of the principle of replicability which in turn underlies the principle of inference. However, what the principle of replicability is aiming at is none other than the repetition of the inference in its original form. In this way, the principle of reproducibility is a point of view (as Popper would say) that logically and by chance precedes the repetition of the original inference. The possibility of running through the inferences is already given by a replicating structure, replicative of the proceedings of the analysis. All this can occur because scientific work is the prisoner of the deductive method.

It is curious that one should be surprised in the face of the natural heterogeneousness of biographies (as differentiated experiences which express different capacities for totalization). Is this not perhaps the authentic condition of human existence? That there should then be biographies which express the totalization of the whole of a society is as mistaken as arguing that one can enclose the whole meaning of a life (if only in some aspects) in a questionnaire. Wishing to bring this reasoning to a climax, one can say that not even from the biography of a sociologist can one summarize society (leaving aside the methods used). Biographies, however, give that sense of place in life which can be constructed in no other way. Biographies allow one to reach those cultural frameworks within which knowledge of oneself and of the other interact. In gathering biographies one has the insertion of the researcher in the context "of a process of historical transmission in which past and present are continually synthesised" (H. G. Gadamer, *Veritá e metodo*, p. 340). The understanding of any text (even a biographic one) is a creative process in which the researcher improves the knowledge of himself by perfecting the knowledge of others. What is thus brought out is the image of cultural frameworks ("life forms") between which a mediation is possible, but only by having available a methodology of adequate understanding. Access to localized biographies is a cognitive necessity and also the proving ground for mediations between cultural frameworks—that of the two co-involved social subjects (a concrete social actor and the researcher or researchers). This closer relationship creates a further bond or condition of adequacy of understanding, but it does not represent a threat to the objectivity of sociological analysis.

As regards inference or measurement, the subject is that of the plausibility of qualitative methods in the context of the social sciences. However, what must first of all be made plausible is the legitimacy of the models of explanation with a quantitative basis, that is, of models in which measurement is used. In scientific work there is generally a (rapid) passage from the qualitative immediacy of the social facts to the introduction of criteria of measurement. This passage is not always desirable, and even if it is, it is never a simple journey. This passage from quality to quantity is determined, obviously, by goals of forecasting. It should here be stressed that forecasting is not the sole aim of the social sciences and sociology. The study of the morphogenesis of any phenomenon or group of phenomena—which is perhaps the most important goal of the social sciences—cannot take place through the use of a model based on measurement precisely because not all the relations are measurable. As G. G. Granger (Modena congress) points out, in the analysis of forms one must complete three actions: identify a phenomenon in its totality and break it down into the parts that structure it (the phase of description); establish comprehension; to include the fact-system in a system of facts where it is possible to determine the origin, stability, and decline of the fact in question.

This cognitive process always has a provisional value (it implies continuous re-totalizations of the three levels). The use of qualitative model, as well as completing the three phases of the explanation, helps an adequate objectivation of the phenomenon in question. Only after this objectivation by qualitative method can one think of introducing criteria of measurement, even though it is difficult to establish when that is possible.

Regarding sociological analysis some words of warning are necessary. The image of analysis as analysis that follows the gathering of the data makes one think of the person who when reading a novel decides *a priori* to leave the understanding of the novel itself to the end. This choice is unfortunately present in a whole specific research methodology.

The dilemma can be summed up in the opposition between movement (the reality one is experiencing) and the state (the reality experienced). It is generally believed only the latter can be an object of knowledge and that it alone is comprehensible.

The example of the reading of the novel, taken from Giddens, is again useful:

Reading a novel involves the understanding of each chapter as one arrives at it, arriving at a never more complete awareness of the whole plot of the book. Thus the understanding of the novel in its entirety is deepened by grasping within it specific sequences: but this greater overall understanding in turn makes possible a fuller appreciation of the specific episodes described as the story proceeds (Giddens, *New rules of sociological method*, pp. 72–73).

Precisely because in the knowledge of the social the relation is between subjects (each with his own frame of reference), the understanding of the social phenomena by the researcher always requires their *pre*-comprehension, which acts as a springboard towards a more adequate understanding. The passage from the simple to the complex and thence to the simple, from the particular to the general and vice versa, from the local to the global and vice versa, from one frame of reference to another and vice versa, happens through an activity of pre-comprehension–comprehension that generates society itself and the categories used to study it. This method of proceeding, which is the essence of the hermeneutic double circle, should be rethought in the light of what is today being stated about the structure of thought, that it is a dialectical, essential unity of induction and deduction, seen as necessary moments of the global activity of the intelligence. In this context, deciding beforehand what is being sought is never a logical *a priori* (which can be faced in an exclusively deductive manner). On the other hand one cannot accept a schema for checking knowledge in which facts confirm facts. The regressive-progressive method is already inside this recognition of the unity of the two moments of knowledge. Rather, it is question of proving and cross-checking the methodological content with those of the hermeneutic method and of knowledge as global activity.

THE IMPOSSIBLE SYNTHESIS

I see I am forced here to take a step backwards. After so many attempts at impersonality, after humbly kneeling beside things in the effort to hear their essential, profound voice, beyond the garrulous chatter and the shadow of an irritating, overpowering ego, I am forced to do a kind of psycho-philosophical strip-tease. I dare hope the exercise does not seem shameless to the demanding reader. I am convinced that the highest heroism an author is capable of lies in his concerning himself with questions before which he, as a person, counts for nothing. Moreover, I am convinced that the inferiority of the moderns lies in their evident inability to forget themselves as individuals. They seem to believe that the sun rises every morning only to light up their windows.

However, it is possible, given the nature of the essay, to make this mixture of existential experience and attempted conceptual rigor. I am aware of how much impurity can be concealed in this mixture. Yet it is an illusion that an essay be an eternal discourse on specific problems, that it should start from rigorous premises and then arrive like a train whose route has been duly decided and mapped at the outset at certain—necessary and necessitating—conclusions, basically intemporal and schematic. This problematic knot has already been grasped and expressed quite clearly:

Whoever is prepared to write an essay declares himself ready at the same time for a work of understanding and interpretation. In this process there are at work a series of elements of a psychological and emotional kind. Impulse, joy, play, imagination are elements of the new "objectivity" the essay brings into being. Through its cognitive impulsion, the essay escapes the typical schemas of historical gnoseologies. It refuses the historic distinction between levels of scientific knowledge and pre-scientific knowledge, whereby it would perhaps be relegated to the second order. . . . It does not accept the rules of the game as set out by science and organized theory whereby, as Spinoza said, the order of things coincides with the order of ideas. And as the compact order of concepts is not identical with existence, the essay does not aim at closed constructs of an inductive, nor of a deductive, type.[15]

Moreover, one thinks with the whole person: brain and blood, mind and nerves. The ancient, venerable dispute between body and soul, on which Christianity was reared, as well as the fascinating Platonic invention of the pure spirit and the good-in-itself, tend in reality to dissolve when they are presented as an object for critical reflection, so that Catholic moral theology itself seems directed today towards a recovery of "bodiliness."[16]

Critical reflection thus departs from, and involves, the whole individual, his reality as unitary reality. The biographical datum is fused with the conceptual schema. Every book, every argument is also an adventure. Before being a system, it has been the fate of a person, a moment of his development, a call. Why, then, life histories? Why, after mastering the quantitative techniques in their now traditional form, especially in North American culture, was I led to give special weight to biographical materials? What dissatisfaction pushed me? Or, in positive terms, what new synthesis was I striving for? The biographical datum is a poor, chipped thing when compared with the calm, impersonal character of theoretical knowledge. Yet it is still true that the experience can still appear as the crack, the fragment from which one may rise up to the globality of the human meaning of the person, the totality of meaning which expresses his intentionality. To understand this point fully, one would need to reexamine in all its significance the concept of production as a human undertaking, in the sense of a founding undertaking of the human—in Hegel before Marx, and in his philosophy of praxis. ("What man is, coincides with his production"· in other words, man as a self-producing and self-relating being, or the human being as *animal confabulans*). This is certainly well outside the conceptions—more or less coherently intellectualist and technocratic—that run from the *homo sapiens* of the Socratic-Cartesian type, to the *homo faber* of the utilitarian-economist tradition, and up to the instinct of efficiency or instinct of workmanship that seems to underlie the variegated sociology and cultural anthropology of Thorstein Veblen.

In 1950, when I was preparing for my trip to the United States after my stays in London and Paris, with that quixotic spirit and sense of destiny which often seem to inspire young provincials setting off to conquer the world, I was moved by the extraordinary ambition, which, however, seemed wholly natural, of joining together the systematic European theoresis and North American techniques of empirical research. Looking back on the situation, I can now say that there was hidden in that purpose my personal Scipio's dream. Today I take from it a substantial lesson in modesty.[17] Possibly, for a good understanding of the orientations and characteristics of a discipline, one must keep in mind its genesis, manners, and also its caprices, the chance nature of its development. A science, like a political movement, an institution, and even an individual, is what it has been. I have already remarked elsewhere that only a disembodied conception of science can entertain the doubt that it has no history, and instead is worked out in the pure sequence of truths arrived at successively through the accumulation of purely rational insights, basically ahistorical and intemporal. It is true that the historical discourse is defined on the basis of its internal self-correctability, in contrast to the religious or the poetic discourses.

However, it is equally true that around the specific scientific truths, such things as schools, groups, and loyalty to the masters are formed. Thus the development of a science is never a smooth progression, but also a history of plots, clashes, power, and blood. In the Summer 1982 number of the *Revue française de sociologie*, there appears an instructive polemical exchange between Carlo G. Rossetti and Diana Pinto on contemporary Italian sociology. Rossetti rebukes it for not having resumed contacts and come to terms with pre-fascist Italian sociology, for which some names are provided, including those of scholars especially active in the fascist decades. The obvious difficulty of establishing contact with a discipline rapidly liquidated in the first years of this century is passed over in silence, almost without a blow, by Crocean idealist reaction.

The real problem of this postwar sociology was to understand the reasons for the extreme methodological and material weakness of pre-fascist Italian sociology before the iron breastplates of Crocean criticism, itself pathetically disarmed regarding the more recent methodological tendencies, from neopositivism to symbolic logic and linguistics, and victorious only because it was involuntarily protected by the fascist autarchy and helped by the cultural closures this necessarily involved. It is enough to read carefully the plan of work with which I started the publication of the *Quaderni-di sociologia* at the beginning of 1951, with the collaboration of Nicola Abbagnano and the publishing house of Marian Taylor, to see that sociology as a science at the criticial level was still considered nonexistent in Italy. This was because of the luxuriant idealist dictatorship, actually promoted by the fascist dictatorship.[18] But something similar also existed in the United States, because of the paleo-positivism dominant there, and thus the proliferation of studies as numerous as they were disjointed, fragmentary, and ultimately useless (one thinks of the precious volume *Knowledge, for What?* by Robert S. Lynd), to which that inadequate theoretical structure inevitably led.

This initial reflection, which was to broaden out, through *La sociologia come partecipazione* (Taylor, Turin 1961) into the setting out of an alternative sociological proposal twenty years later (*Una sociologia alternativa*, Bari, 1972), has often been misunderstood and interpreted as a kind of *mea culpa*. This is certainly a very Italian, Catholic attitude, in specific circumstances respectable, but quite misplaced here, especially for one who would see in the champions of juridical formalism the saviors of sociology. For it is hard to deny that especially in immediate postwar Europe and in cultural and political situations both deeply immobile and paralysed into meanly defensive reactions, sociology presented itself as a coherent, radical revolt against formalism. Today, especially for scholars of the younger generation, it seems equally difficult to evaluate realistically the difficulties faced by the first sociologists, particularly in Italy, enclosed in a still static, confessional society, and a culture more interested in the *bel canto* of formal systematics than the toughness, patient and worn, of empirical field research. It is also true that French scholars too— think, for two exemplary cases, of Michel Crozier and Alain Touraine—though able to count on the rich and living heritage of Durkheim, had to emigrate and form themselves in the United States.

I understand how natural the rebuke for having gone overseas to seek what is probably available at home may appear. I do not forget the amazement of G. K. Chesterton's traveller, when from the ship's deck he finally saw a spit of land, hailed it and, relieved, awaited the delights of new world; when he came closer to shore his euphoria was tempered: he began to recognize the outlines, see the familiar ports and villages: it was dear old England! Of my stay in the United States I have written at length elsewhere, especially in the preface to the second edition of *Lineamenti di sociologia* (Liguori, Naples 1976). I repeat that rather than to Chesterton's traveller I should refer myself to that fine piece by Cicero, *Somnium Scipionis*. Scipio the Elder describes for his nephew Emilianus the advantages of the synthesis between Roman practicality and Greek speculative ability. In the 1950s I hoped to be able to provide the great tradition of classical European sociological thought, and enrich it by adding to it the methodological instruments latterly developed in the United States. Today, I can say that the attempt failed. There is a meta-technical moment in any research that cannot be omitted. Techniques are not theoretically indifferent. They are not neutral. They are not a kind of free port, nor can they be considered as interchangeable, or applied at will to any problem whatever.

The questions with which sociological analysis is involved are historically conditioned. They require the calibration of technical instruments of research. One needs a critical acclimatization that goes beyond the supposed neutrality of methodological procedures. Only a bleached methodology can escape the weight of implicit, built-in values. But the price is high. It corresponds to the loss of the historical consciousness of the problems. It involves emptying the research. It falls into the unconscious quantification of the qualitative. Then we have the curious inversion of priorities. Exact measurement takes over the basic cognitive role, whilst its function is firstly instrumental, subordinate, and secondary to the general orienting hypotheses and specific working hypotheses. Finally one knows everything, very precisely, but no longer about what and for what. The sense of the problem has collapsed along with historical awareness. The research wanders in a void. At the most it confirms speculatively the givenness of the existing. It cannot effectively grasp the dynamics of the development of phenomena and the sense of direction of historical movement, the nature and rhythm of social change.

At this point life-histories are a basic escape. They bring back sociological research to its origins and primary goal: empirical analysis, conceptually oriented, of human facts as phenomena in constant tension, as fluid realities producing meaning, relatively determined but at the same time unpredictable. For this reason, they are dramatic, never *a priori* mechanically determined as paleo-positivism and panlogistic idealism believe. Nor can they be congealed into essentialist concepts, closed, given once and for all.

THE PERSONAL EQUATION

From the studies of the commune of Castellamente (see nos. 1–3 of *Quederni di sociologia* 1951) the biographical datum seemed to me the basic raw material of sociological analysis, as it did not propose to confine itself to the level, however worthy, of sociography. However, the biographical approach was to reveal itself in all its importance in *La piccola città* (Milan, Comunitá 1959), where autobiographical testimonies already helped to make known in depth—beyond what the researchers suspected—the hidden society. This refers not only, and not so much, to the formal structure of institutions, as the effective manner, the everyday quality and style of their functioning. These already made sufficiently clear, had by chance the cultural and political ruling class been less deaf, the limits of the rationalizing ability of capitalism. Here, while the analysis holds good for the whole of Southern Italy and the islands, not only has capitalism not rationalized the social process, but rather the social process and traditional community have "levantized" capitalism. The great Mediterranean mother has defeated the austere shade of John Calvin.

I have already remarked (see the preface to the second edition, Naples: Liguori, 1973) that the documentation and the interpretation of this inverted process require research techniques that fall outside ideological programs and political projects. Mid-range and microsociological studies are needed. However, it is hardly necessary to warn that the ideal task should lie in the concrete, or empirically checkable, demonstration of the dialectical interplay between the micro-and

macro-levels. I noted at the time that regarding this particular point one should record the failure of sociological research,
which is either micro-sociological, very aware of the empirical, and rigorously checked quantitatively but conceptually
weak, unverifiable, and thus unable to link concepts with empirical indicators, and thus still in the traditional sense philosophical: or else it is a simple projection of suggestions,
impressions, preferences; or again, it is antipathies, irrational
prophecies, or even ingenious theoretical constructs, nonetheless compromised regarding their internal coherence in terms
of the undeclared, personal assumptions of the individual researcher.

In this regard I refer to the book by Dominique Schnapper,
L'Italie rouge et noire (Paris: Gallimard, 1971), centering on
the city of Bologna, and aiming at discovering and interpreting the weight of ancestral tradition on the collective behavior of Italians, independently, against or beyond specific political beliefs, religious affiliations, education, income, profession,
or social class. The hypothesis was plain: to discover, beneath
the variety and the even striking contrasts, a common denominator that expressed itself in strong homogeneity and a basically convergent lifestyle. What did Schnapper bring into
lifestyle? Ways of dressing, typical reactions in cases of family
mourning, family ceremonies and rights, furnishings (entrance hall, the varnished kitchen, the lounge, bedroom fur-
niture, the dressing-table, etc.). The essence of the lifestyle
was provided by the immediate elements of the everyday. In
her view, these elements are common to all Italians, as they
have never seriously been questioned, because the political
and ideological struggle, though it may take on heated tones,
never goes deep enough to touch them. Hence, despite innovative noises, the deeply and invincibly conservative and
philistine character of Italian society, even in Bologna, the
supposed center of revolutionary experiences, the stronghold
of communism, arises.

In this sense, as it seemed then, and as I still think today,
it was necessary that the macro-sociological level, though basic, should not remain empty, but rather be filled with the
content of information and interpretation that close-up socio-

logical analysis, with its instruments of direct enquiry and research seen as an interpersonal relation, can give. However it is clear that, in that research, biographies still had a purely illustrative function as regards predetermined arguments concerning the breakdown of a community assailed by economic and social development of a technocratic kind: that is, a development conceived and activated as a unilateral process from above downwards, from center to periphery, like a neo-colonial enterprise of technological imperialism. Basically, it is like an operation of paramilitary engineering, which a fine patina of sociability manages to make functional, both as lubricant and alibi, and also as masking of the simple fact that a land designated as a place of mission to be redeemed is in reality unknown regarding its original characteristics and treated as a zone for plunder. As in Thomas and Znaniecki's *The Polish Peasant*, the biographical data in *La piccola città* help to illustrate an assumed argument, built on the knowledge already possessed by the authors. In *Vite di baraccati*, *Giovani e droga*, and *Vite di periferia*, the biographical data, on the other hand, have a cognitive function in the full sense, and are the irreplaceable instruments to bring out the problems and cultural themes that matter. In the case of the addicts they are in fact the only means we have to manage to listen to people and groups whose marginality and illegality block the road to normal procedures for selecting a representative sample, according to the formal rules of traditional quantitative methods.

But how are biographical testimonies collected? Once collected, how does one proceed? One of the most fascinating aspects of the work of research through qualitative methods lies in the fact that there is not a tested methodology, a kind of formula to apply according to the instructions for use for every case examined. The researcher who uses life histories is forced to follow the example of the classics and build his research instruments in the real process of research itself, in direct contact with the problems he has decided to tackle. In this sense, it should be said that qualitative methods are in the first instance driven by a cognitive scientific purpose, but that their ultimate justification lies basically in a meta-theoretical option of a moral kind, related to the conception of science as a human enterprise, tending to resolve problems and questions of society. It is one based on an attitude of respect and attention towards people. The latter are ends or values in themselves, who cannot be used instrumentally, nor for cognitive ends, without risking their objectualization, or denying them as persons.

The researcher tends to defend his status as professional in the real or narrow sense of research. The professional is defended by the specific knowledge of his *Fach*. He is a specialist who speaks his own esoteric language, uses mysterious formulas that the common herd don't understand; the common people, that is, who ask for his services. He is part of a priestly caste that bases its power and possible social privilege on this asymmetry. This complex of attitudes may serve the normal professions in a technically advanced society, but cannot be adapted to sociology, at the risk of its falling into sociographic reportage or a police-type report.

Between researcher and object of research there is a link that cannot be denied without endangering the critical character of the analysis. It is here that the old prejudice of paleo-positivism roosts: the temptation of emulating the natural sciences or the so-called exact sciences in what they today recognize as a caricature of science, an undue restriction on the meaning and importance of knowledge and the downgrading of science to scientism. What has been so long seen and interpreted as the reason for sociology's inferiority and the human sciences appears today as the reason for their primacy, the internal source of their critical nature. A social researcher cannot study social classes at the critical level without initially socially and historically placing himself, and without questioning himself about *his* social class. Every researcher is also always an object of research. His objectivity lies in recognizing and making explicit his principles of personal preference. I have already elsewhere clarified this basic point.[19]

The social sciences have the same scientific qualifications as those the sciences of nature can count on. But that does not justify their summary identification. The personal equation of the scholar in the natural sciences lies in a quantitatively measurable distortion of the senses so that his knowledge allows the elimination of correction of errors in observation. But what of the social scientist? Wherein lies his personal equation? One thing is certain, that whether he be near- or far-sighted, or that his reading time of a certain instrument is fast or slow, means very little in the direction of his research work.

In the sociologist's case, the personal equation involves the qualitative plane. It is an important conquest for contemporary sociology, not so much that it is recognized that sociologists must introduce assumptions into their research, as the demonstration that certain assumptions, necessary value-laden, are inevitable in any sociological research that does not wish to be reduced to a mere undirected accumulation of elementary data. If this is so, what does it mean for the social scientist to resolve the personal equation? Does it not perhaps mean revealing himself to himself? Coming clear regarding his position in society? Recall and emergence of his historical consciousness, not to be confused with the erudition of pure information, which implies instead the determination of historically mature problems, independently and beyond what possibly interests the market and potential customers?

The corollary is a double one: a process of constant self-analysis, and systematic research, inspired as a relation or non-naturalistic, asymmetrical communication with the "other," an acceptance of his otherness and thus a dialogue with actors in the human situation of the object of research, as co-research. It is clear that observer and observed still confront each other, but the two realities are not alien to each other or incompatible. They are placed on a ground of basic parity. The irreplaceable research instrument for the sociologist is then his experience as a social person, or the person who participates wholly in that reality he is investigating. He is able to understand only after listening, on the basis of all his experience, within his personal equation.

THE INTERACTION

Research grows from interaction as an essential assumption that guarantees its non-mechanistic character. Interaction is, on the other hand, essential for the biographical approach;

indeed, it is its distinguishing characteristic. It expresses the challenge of the qualitative along with the insidious charm of narration. But it also involves the interdisciplinary approach to research, which I should prefer to call postdisciplinary, so evident is it now how necessary it is that the subject of the research be globally and coordinatedly tackled by the various human sciences with their specific resources of method and substance. Interaction gives rise to a series of mediations between researcher and narrator first, and, then, in the story itself, the life-history, between self and self-perception, the narrating and the narrated I, in a dialectical tension between presenter, presented, and self-represented. Here, ever thing, from the lapsus, so important in orality, the gesture, the facial expressions, and the subjects dwelt on, makes for consistency; plot, process of transition from individual history to collective constructs, from individual idiosyncracy to collective behavior and modes of social control.

There are no rules for interaction. Every researcher makes his own. Nuto Rivelli tells his subject everything at once. What you say will be a book. But he adds: The book is not all the research, the book is a product, and often the fruit of a painful compromise with market requirements, the preferences of the publisher, and so on. The research, rather, is in the first place a meeting, an interaction. He makes a rather wide approach to the book.

Maurizio Catani spoke to a single person, *Tante Suzanne*, in four in-depth conversations, and from a single life-history brought out an instructive social history through orality, breaking down the usual gaps between the different areas of a life: work, family, etc. He managed admirably to restore the unity of the living person. In *Vite di baraccati* I acted as a solitary researcher, establishing a relation of trust with my witnesses. I had no single interlocutor; there was a group. From this experience I got the idea of constructing the biography of a primary group, as groups too live, grow, change, and die. When I arrived at Pina and Salvatore's shack, in the founding family of the shanty-town of Acquedotto Felice, I sat beside the gas stove, put the recorder in the middle of the wobbly table that was the center of the furnishings, and we began to converse. At times the voices overlapped. The transcription would be difficult. I would use normal punctuation, with some bracketing, as in theater parts. But I have the impression that more refined contrivances, like those tried worthily by Renato Cavallaro, suffer from being labored, compensated only partially for the average reader by the advantages of rigor. Naturally, orthographic transcription, rather than orthophonic, using a dash to mark pauses in the discourse goes beyond the simple technical level and marks the extraordinary care he lends "to the different phonological, lexical, morpho-syntactic and rhetorico-ideological levels of the spoken language, explored with constant reference to the standard models of oral, subordinate expression, but also inserted with full right in the concrete analysis of the specific structures of *those* life histories."[20]

However, when and if it may be possible to replicate the research of *Vite di baraccati* I think I should give the reader less meager information on the practices followed, the dialectic between Pina and Salvatore, and between them and the primary group of the neighbors, the way I managed to make myself accepted, the relation of trust which however does not exclude critical distance, the times of the conversations, involvement of acquaintances, friends, passers-by, so that the circle enlarged beyond the narrow family group that, to Oscar Lewis, on the contrary, should be considered as the natural unit of research. I believe my silence on these aspects during the study has a deeper meaning than simple forgetfulness. Bearing in mind that the framework of relations between interviewer and interviewee remain one of the hardest problems of biographical method, it seems arguable that I tried to hide from myself and the reader the effects of the research process on myself and my attitudes. I tried to remove myself from the effects of interaction. It is clearly easier to theorize it than live it. I also understand better how many researchers prefer the anonymous questionnaire and its boxes, yes—no—don't know. It is more straightforward, more hygienic, more ascetic. One is never called to task. It is a pity that in this way the research never touches the ground, is at once precise and insignificant. The problematic has been well grasped, also in its paradoxic aspects: being content with statements made without going back to the implicit and explicit motives which lay at the base of the research, without studying the process of interaction which had given rise to these results, may seem an act of respect for the observed, while in reality, as we pointed out earlier, it reduces him to a simple, inanimate object of research.

In this sense, the choice of the biographical method in contrast to traditional sociological research is disturbing. It asserts the centrality of personal relations. There will be complaints about the violation of scientific method. But what is science if not a public proceeding? Isn't this publicness satisfied perhaps whenever the researcher at the outset declares his values, completes his historical and political self-placement, and defines himself as a social being regarding the problem the research will deal with, and makes clear the tools and stages of his enquiry? Another interpretation is possible. There is an understandable psychological resistance from the researchers in putting themselves at risk.

Reading these histories [referring to *Vite di periferia*] I realized they give information not only on the interviewee but also on the interviewer, on his way of relating to others, his ability to immerse himself in a marginal situation, on his knowledge of the situation he is investigating, and on the relevance of the questions posed. The method of life histories is very sincere—and dangerous—*because it forces us to reveal ourselves*, it does not allow us to hide behind the claimed scientificity and neutrality of so-called objective instruments. It reveals that sociological and psychological research is a relation between persons.[21]

The interaction poses more complex problems when the research is conducted not by a single researcher but by a group.[22] It is not only a matter of the difficulty of the multidisciplinary research, and hence the different language, conceptual instruments, and tradition of the various disciplines. The acceptance of the consequences of interaction may take place in different ways and create problems of harmony within the research group itself. One advantage seems obvious, on the other hand, regarding the reliability of the transcriptions. The recording is not always clear, especially when there are noises, overlaid voices, words of dubious meaning. The reconstruction of the dialogue or collective interview is certainly helped by the presence of two or more researchers. If one collects the biographical accounts of a primary group and not of an individual it is almost essential to be able to count on a team. There is a natural division of labor. If a researcher speaks, the other can note down gesture, background, environment, happenings in the course of the interview. If one is seated round a table with several people one can use several recorders placed at opposite corners, with people responsible for each area. In this case the recordings after transcription can be compared and possibly integrated. The risk of losing important parts of the discussion can thus be lessened—a risk increased, as those experienced in field work know, by such contingent factors as a baby crying, traffic noise, or dogs barking. Among the various systems of recording, the tape seems clearly preferable as it permits the documentation of the delivery of the phrase, the recurring adjective, the idiomatic expression, pauses, and silences. It is amazing how much one learns from rehearing the recording of a conversation from which one believed one had learned everything there was to learn. The interlocutors themselves, in rehearing themselves often seem amazed and ask, "Did I really say this?" It may be the start of a *prise de conscience*, the critical grasp and conscious rerun of their own life experience.

It is thus clear that to recount one's own life is not necessarily an idyll. It is a risky and often painful operation. The interaction it involves is almost never a gift to auspicious circumstances. Intention, language, gesture, subjects, memory, structure of emergent meanings: a life history is not only a sequence of happenings, but a world that develops and unfolds under our eyes, in our ears, between our hands. I have always nurtured and involuntarily fed a religious sense in myself while gathering autobiographical testimonies, a feeling touching on the fear of profanation. The interlocutor is not simply an object of research but a human being, trusting, who puts his life in your hand. In no other situation is knowledge such a potential instrument of domination. Prepared for and accepted in its ultimate consequences, interaction guarantees the state of parity between researcher and researched and satisfies a moral need which is at the same time the essential presupposition for a correct cognitive enterprise. However, the researcher does not always manage to establish himself, directly, the necessary contacts with the potential interlocutors. There are subtle and often almost impassable barriers to overcome.

Every gatherer of life-histories has the common experience that women at the start of the encounter are uneasy and mostly ask that their husband be present. This is not just mistrust. It is the natural reluctance to disclose oneself, to say the things which at most one thinks of, which one does not say even to oneself. So, one asks for one's husband to be present. However, if one also manages to see the women alone, subjects and problems come out that would not have been mentioned or dealt with in his presence. Thus Maria in the Valle Aurelia studies, in an uncontradictory fashion, first wanted the presence of her husband and then, when speaking alone with the researchers, said that every evening the situation was the same: "either fuck or kicks." Thus it is often necessary to have an intermediary, a privileged go-between, a kind of second-level interaction.

Other means of interaction have been used by researchers to overcome the shyness of potential informants. One knows that the co-author of *The Polish Peasant* had an announcement published in which he offered a small cash payment for every letter from an immigrant. Miguel Barnet, author of the well-known *Autobiography of a Slave*, said explicitly: "At the start he spoke to me of his personal problems: pension, women, health. I tried to resolve some of them for him. I gave him little presents: cigars, badges, photographs. He related in a jumbled manner, and with no chronological order, important episodes in his life." Probably Barnet's interlocutor behaved like Mark Twain when he dictated his biography from his bed, where he lay much of the time, following the simple association of ideas, without at all concerning himself with the chronological succession of events, and indeed brilliantly anticipating the Joycean narrative technique of stream of consciousness.

However, Barnet continued in his explanation that these were very useful: "Even though I worked out my basic questions according to ethnological texts and questionnaires, it was the practice to bring out those most directly linked to the life of the informant." This is the practice of research, using habit, the direct relation, familiarity, the recognition of the other as other. Little by little, Esteban, the slave, not only chose the important subjects himself, but suggested aspects forgotten or omitted by the researcher, forcing him to broaden the perspective of the research, enriching its problematic context, making it a point of intersection for many disciplines, from history to literature. Barnet wrote:

Many of our sessions were recorded on tape. This let me familiarize myself more with his forms of language, phrases, syntax, archaisms and turns of speech. The need to check facts, dates, and other details, led me to talk with old men more or less the same age. . . . I used reference works, the proceedings of the town councils of Cienfuegos and Remedios, and carefully re-examined that period so as not to fall into historical errors in putting questions. Even though, as is clear, my work is not historical. There is history because the life of a man is involved.

Again, later, Barnet, like all collectors of life-histories, found himself coming to terms with the problem of transcription—a difficult stage of the research where one completes the complex transition from orality to writing—two different media of communication linked to clearly opposing logics. Barnet's solution, healthily pragmatic, perhaps too unconcerned, was not for literal transcription: "Had I faithfully reported his words, the book would have been too difficult and full of repetitions. However, I was especially concerned to preserve the syntax, when it was necessary." His intention was not that of writing a novel, nor yet of setting out a traditional type of ethnological essay. "This book just tells of the vicissitudes which ethnology collects for studies of the social environment, for historical and folkloristic purposes. Our greatest satisfaction is to relate them through the mouth of a genuine protagonist of the Cuban historical process."[23]

At this point it is hardly necessary to remark that, valuable though machines are, not everything can be left to them. Participant observation is a preliminary, basic operation as a direct, personal contact. Not only this, as I said in *History and Life-Histories*; one does not tell one's own *Erlebnis* to a tape-recorder. There are also reasons of practical heuristic convenience. It is good to take notes during the recording so as not to lose significant details of the total picture, and the climate in the group as it has been forming. For example, at this point Tom got up and left, Dick made a signal to shut someone up, Harry nodded or made eloquent signs of disapproval and denial. One must in addition re-order the notes as soon as possible, in any case before forgetting the circumstances that made up the background and context of the recording. It is unwise to trust one's memory. For researchers, memory is a facility that forgets.

On the other hand I must remark that the idea of attempting the biography not of an individual, nor even of a single family as a natural nuclear group, but rather of a relatively fluid primary group, so as to grasp the process of socialization of the individual in his becoming concrete, did not just come to me from a theoretical excursus, or particularly after some criticial demands I made of Oscar Lewis's work. It originated in the practice of field research, especially at Acquedotto Felice and later at Valle Aurelia, where I had found it impossible to isolate my interlocutor and myself in a relatively protected environment, as it was there, moreover, that the conception and still more the experience of privacy of the purely urban-bourgeois kind was practically unknown. Further, many years before, at the start of the studies on urban marginality in the Roman periphery, what might have seemed an original theoretical discovery was also dictated if not imposed by the meagerness of the financial means available to the researchers, which at most could pay for the bus ticket to take them to the terminus where the public transport network stopped and these para-urban settlements began, in Rome as in Rio or Santiago del Chile or Buenos Aires (under the most various titles—

outskirts, shanty-towns, bidonvilles, favelas, villas miserias, barriadas, poblaciones).[24] Seeing I could not isolate the interlocutor of the moment, it was worth considering making the whole group the interlocutor. More worked out and perhaps more civilly literary seemed the technique of Lewis, who in turn had used the system of the multiple interview whereby, for example, the same episode was recounted, as in the film *Rashomon*, by the different children and the father in such a way and according to different interpretations with results sometimes parallel and at others conflicting.[25]

In *Vite di periferia* a new road was tried. It has been justly remarked that here was an attempt to report the dialogue as closely possible to the original conversations. This means one adheres to the real lengths of the conversations, at times involving not the whole span of a life, but rather individual moments of it. No wonder the reading is rather difficult. The materials, not re-ordered, are often boring, repetitive, and non-linear. These are typical inconveniences of orality, but the often repeated subjects make one suspect specially sensitive nuclei. The hesitations, the lapsus, the return of certain phrases, have their symptomatic importance. It is clear that even the most faithful transcriptions have their limits. Whoever had taken part personally in the conversation then wrote the report, a kind of court record of the interview, looking after the punctuation, remembering a possible pause, a hesitation, the lowering and raising of the voice, and so on. The interventions of the researchers are recorded in italics so the reader can orient himself more easily. Naturally the limitations of the oral character of the writing-down remain—the gestures, the background, climate, and ambiance of the encounter.

The procedure followed is different from that used by Oscar Lewis or earlier by Thomas and Znaniecki, very interested in the re-ordering of the material even though they did not clearly make the criteria explicit. It also differs from those of Revelli, who shows with dots and brackets the author's contributions, jumps in the narrative that seem linear and develop in a chronological order, what is in Italian, not dialect, though with some specifically significant phrases left in Piedmontese. At any rate, the author's interventions do not appear in the narrative. In *Vite di periferia* there is no claim to achieve an impossible objectivity that would have re-introduced the worst elements of paleo-positivism. As regards others of my studies, like *Studi e ricerche sul potere*,[26] the method was inverted. From longitudinal research on a stratified sample of Romans with a complex questionnaire I moved to a study based on the refusal of the systematic, where the subjects were approached through friends, perhaps at the *Casa del popolo*, a meeting-place and place of relaxation with a considerable historical reputation in the wake of the anti-fascist and socialist movement, especially in the afternoon and evening of Saturdays and Sundays. Around the table where the researchers sat with the recorder, the interlocutors could change, interrupt, contradict one another, and take up a discussion left hanging.[27]

The recorder is thus not a point of departure but of arrival, and not only does not exclude but rather requires other means of study and observation, aside from the basic moment of participant observation: for example, the study of the historical documents of the municipal archives,[28] ecological and territorial analysis, the use of photography,[29] content analysis of local newspapers, the administration of special socio-psychological tests. Anyway, before arriving at the tape-recorder, a considerable investment of time and various preparatory activities, such as meetings, meals, and afternoons and evenings spent together, are required: all that "propedeutic conviviality" that seems a luxury to the sociologist true to the market and its rules, for whom time is money, whereas they are essential activities for the social scientist conscious first of all of having to deal with human beings. It is this detail that escapes the sociographers and the sociological brokers who apply to research on the human the same efficientistic criteria of current managerial activity. In conclusion, interaction is basic for the biographical approach and is in its essence a pact of trust[30] between the researchers and the informants, which binds the parties to reciprocal respect and a common cognitive undertaking, which cannot, however, be imposed and realized surreptitiously, but rather must be accepted and carried forward by both sides and in a situation of essential parity.

CONTEXT AND TEMPORALITY

Some eager followers of the biographical method fall into an error comparable to that of the quantifying sociologists, who, armed with their cards and rigid questionnaires, do not find it opportune to dive into the wide ocean of objectivity, being also obsessed, one must say, by the time-limits imposed by their hirers. The former seem impatient to collect juicy autobiographical evidence and do not seem to have time to consider initially, but with great care, the context or specific historical framework where the autobiographical account is situated, with its basic economic, social, political, and cultural components. It is therefore necessary at this point to make a logico-linguistic definition of the terms used. Terms such as life-history, life story, biography, autobiography, social history, and psychohistory are used interchangeably, but we are dealing with strongly differentiated terminologies and semantics, which also serve different ends in the field of research undertaken through the use of biographical materials. Naturally, orality is prevalent. However, one should not omit to mention the lives of more or less famous characters, or their autobiographies, from Augustine to Rousseau, Cellini, Mark Twain, Vittorio Alfieri, and so on. They are important stages, at different levels, as witness of the interest in affairs of the ego. But, for our theme, orality is basic in that initially the autobiography is dictated, in various ways collected, then written down elsewhere by the interviewer with all the questions posed in the delicate passage from the spoken to the written word, from the logic of orality to that of writing. To transcribe the oral always and inevitably means reducing, interpreting, and translating. To what point, and with what criteria? Listening speaks. The silence of listening is as active as the words of the witness.

But how many researchers, maturing in the culture of competitive self-affirmation and social self-promotion, really know how to listen? On the other hand, faithfulness to orality is certainly not passive. Moreover, in the written version, when we accept the current punctuation, we already confer meaning. Nuto Revelli resolves the problem at its roots. He clearly distinguishes between research and book. On his books he sets an exclusive right. When a witness speaks too much, he has gone over the edge, as he said recently, and it is he who steps in and cuts: "He has told me everything. And then, out of respect, I must cut." Out of respect? Can one censor out of respect? It is a difficult point. I cut nothing. I only cut if the mass of testimonies endangers their publication, that is, their social utility as effective instruments for unmasking the hidden society. In me the logic of understanding and demystifying prevails over the ethic that crosses its legs. But every position, clearly, is legitimate. The essential thing is that the researcher be aware of it.

The predominance of orality legitimates the now common use of the category of oral history. However, within this category one must use subtle, basic distinctions. One must know how to acclimatize critically, to put in context. We find ourselves before the whole oral tradition as a great collective heritage, but from this—which one could still confuse with folklore as popular culture—there is, clearly separated the oral source, the individual testimony, which can be person-actor or document, and which in turn bursts out into life-history or life-story (*récit de vie*). Life-history is the direct testimony of a whole cycle of existence, a *Lebenslauf*, a whole autobiographical account, whereas the life-story is an oddment of life, the story of an episode, particularly meaningful in the narrator's view. As a general definition, Lejeune's seems acceptable: "A retrospective story in prose a real person makes of his own existence, when he places the accent on his individual life, in particular the history of his personality."[31]

Acceptable, but far from exhaustive. It is not just a question of distinguishing between a chronological autobiography and one tied to the spontaneous association of ideas and situations independently of the chronological sequence, as mentioned above. The autobiographical account must be inserted in a complete context or framework that also allows the researchers who use the biographic method to proceed to the criticism of the sources, like historians and philologists. In this regard, it is basic to set out clearly the reasons that lead to the dictation or final draft of the autobiography, just as one must distinguish between the autobiography written before the research from that specifically set out for the researcher who requests it. The goals can naturally change; they run from self-defense or evidence of expiation or reparation of wrongs, even moral ones, done to others (from bankrupts to Saint Augustine) to the desire to establish historical truth, or the search of one's own personality and re-ordering of one's own ideas and ideals in life. Here above all it would be right to pay attention to how much distortion and deformation occurs at the moment of speaking, not only because of the prejudices of the witness but also because, in reconstructing his own life, her certainly does not give up contributions owed to his own imaginary creation, often stimulated by the particular characteristics of the culture and society to which he belongs.

The gathering of autobiographical materials, finally, should obey the requirement of a relatively disinterested research into certain facts or periods, or have a scientific purpose not contented with official versions, but rather intent on digging in the lesser-known aspects and in those dimensions of events generally left out or neglected as irrelevant. Then there are the biographies of a person, generally famous, written by others, or again biographies collected by a single researcher but with the aim of illuminating a whole historical phase in its aspects of everyday society (as with *Tante Suzanne*, by M. Catani). To be distinguished from the biography which concerns the whole of a life or much of one, there is the *tranche de vie*, or specific slice of life, which instead tends to clarify in what way a particular traumatic happening has been experienced at the individual and collective level. This concerns how and why this may possibly have changed the habits of people, what reciprocal reaction has been created between the microsociological individual or group level, and the macrosociological structural-institutional one.

Finally, the importance for research of biographical material of the most varied kinds must be recognized, from iconographic documents (photographs and portraits), letters, diaries, accounts, bills, etc., or objects, cultural material, instruments and tools for work and cooking. As has been worthily demonstrated by the studies of Vittorio Dini, these are essential factors for reconstructing daily life, especially when one does not restrict oneself to an external description, but grasps their function symbolically (for example, the symbology of colors). Again, here is outlined the basic difference between the life-history and the free, unstructured interview, or the occasional testimony. For example, the conversations literally recorded in *Vite di periferia* are open testimonies. By putting together and, as it were, attaching these conversations to biographical material already recorded, to information on the context and to knowledge earlier acquired regarding the individuals and primary groups questioned, it is possible to make life histories in the true sense emerge.

In this sense, contextualization is the basic safety net, the network in which the specific life-histories are inserted and framed, taking on all their meaning as precious, invaluable pieces in the general mosaic. The need for contextualization rests on the selective character of the memory of individuals and even the most accurate witnesses. With the passing of time, certain facts and not others not only tend to emerge and dominate, but the so-called memory-screen also exists, and makes its presence felt. The interlocutor wavers between two opposite, symmetric poles: an absence of memories even of elementary facts, distractions, verbal forgetfulness, lapses, uncertainty of recall, weakness of concentration. Or else, excess of memory, with fixation on some special words, phrases, facts, recessive memories, to the point of giving the impression of obsessiveness in memory-contents, segmented, however, and wrenched out of context.[32]

On the other hand, it is hard to protect life-histories and stories from the risk of para-literary novelettishness. Nor can the various testimonies be fully understood unless they can be compared with the average progression and structural characteristics of a given situation. It is only against this contextual background that we can describe and interpret the "interstitial strategies" of individuals and primary groups at grips with officialdom and the system of written, binding rules. The context thus provides indispensable knowledge regrading specific normative field in relation to which there develops real,

specific conduct in the individuals. The fact that many biographical testimonies fall into psychologism or the para-literary is, in my view, to be attributed to a lack of contextualization. This requires a whole, made up of historical, political,
and cultural knowledge, able to allow the construction of the
environmental, social, and family framework in which the biographical fact is inserted and to which it reacts. The relation
of mutual conditioning, to which text and context give rise,
lacks one pole and spins around itself, becoming incomprehensible if contextualization has not been effected rigorously
enough.

It has been usefully remarked that one must give the reader
the referents for understanding. For example,

when Dina Mugnaini said "my family are separated" (*La mi famiglia
si son divisi*) or "We returned to San Donato" (*semo tornati a San
Donato*), she expressed propositions semantically determined by the
peasant-sharecropper society of the estates. The division is not a di-
vorce, but a common practice of farm families, that of the break-up
of the polynuclear, cohabiting family in critical moments of the relation between the productivity of the holding and consumer needs,
and in general when the family becomes too numerous. *Tornati* in
Tuscan means "moved," transferred, or went to live, and here points
to the abandonment of one estate and the passage to another, indicated by name. (In this regard, see the question of emigration in the
first testimonies collected in Piedmont by Nuto Revelli and that of
sex in his more recent book.) This concerns a didactic but crucial
aspect of understanding.[33]

However, it is clear that the context does not cancel out
individual decisions. Indeed, it should be remarked that the
against-the-stream behavior of a person, and thus too the
wearing and bearing down of himself, is difficult to evaluate
except in terms of the current and generally accepted models
and norms. Individual choices and personal motivations must
be taken into consideration in that they enrich the text-con-
text relation, as is actuely shown by the study and comment
of P. Clemente:

Let us take another passage from the text: "*When my mother died,
my sister was married, my elder brother was married. . . . My sister-*

in-law didn't want to stay at home because she didn't want to bring up the family: and I stayed there with my dad, my twin brother and younger sister, so that I had to stay ten years." In this case the note might refer to the essay on "context" which reconstructs the outlines of the farm family, but here should penetrate to more demanding considerations. For example, with a note like this: "It is a central passage of the biography, the description of the state of a family after the death of the mother which, because of individual choices and generational situations, became decisive in Dina's life. For ten years, till her marriage, from 17 years of age, Dina was the "adult" woman in the family, the "housekeeper," and had to manage it. Here there are put together individual choices and motivations, as well as generational states. The result is not due to "tradition" or social "laws" but an interplay of individual tactics. An aspect of the family morphology is defined, graspable only from personal testimonies, and cannot be "deduced" from a model of rules and variations made without an individualized case-study.[34]

Contextualization, on the other hand, can usefully mitigate and in some cases drastically correct the mythologizing fantasy of some informants. Forgetfulness, misunderstandings, partial or distorted memories, even in practical questions, can occur. At Valle Aurelia, for example, the discussions of the former kilnmen about pay are scarcely believable. The figures differ widely, as does the estimate of hours worked. This necessitates a return to the union contracts for the job at the time, and an investigation allowing the reconciling of the discrepancies. To quote a famous example, in Lewis's *Son of Sanchez*, the testimonies of the different brothers and sisters often contradict each other and the father's memories. The reader is faced with parallel histories where he is certainly able to identify the points of difference, but has no basis for comparison. The context is too weak to allow it. An example from literature is that of Virginia Woolf's letters, abundant, detailed, to friends and yet, strangely to us, silent on the war, probably not from lack of concern but rather from a level of concern so common as to make comment superfluous. However, without taking into consideration the fact of the war, a fact that upset and radically changed the style of life, these letters would be incomprehensible.

Another example involves our study at Valle Aurelia. Here, there were many witnesses who stated the valley was visited by Lenin in his time. From archival research it was possible to say the visit was made by the anarchist Malatesta. Independently of the historical exactness of the information, the thing has great significance from the viewpoint of the collective imagination, and when dealing with a community like that of the kilnmen, "red" par excellence, equivalent to that of Roman printers. On the other hand, only an accurate analysis of a historical nature allows one to be aware of and measure the significance of the "invention" of modern witnesses.

Here arises the basic link between context and time, and symmetrically, time and the lived experience. Each context has its specific temporality, its rhythm of evolution, a time of its own movement. On the other hand, every life-history is lived in the framework of its temporality. Life-history in fact permits the understanding of a society on the basis of two elements, essential in its construction: (a) the social actor, and (b) temporality, through which the individual becomes part of history by becoming a social actor. The expression "killing time" is a common one, which the Latins expressed less dramatically in the phrase "*tempus terer*," waste time, as against its fruitful and creative use, "(*tempus redimere*)." Certainly, we can kill time until one day time really does kill us, with death, once and for all. Here there arises, however, with the industrial revolution and the coming of capitalism, Franklin's "time is money," that is, the quiet, almost subterranean beginning, surrounded by an aura of pious devotion, of universal commodification. Lewis Mumford maintained that not the invention of the steam engine but of the clock was the supreme revolutionary invention. Perhaps he was right. Koyré showed that the great watershed of modern history passes through the myth of quantitative precision, the fetishism of exactness that would constrict the surroundings of the validity of knowledge, and make it correspond with that of measurement. It is not just the surprise of the Calabrian immigrants in England when they realized that one goes to work even when it snows.[35] The surprise goes deeper. The time of life, or its duration and quality, whereby an instant may be worth, and compress, a whole cycle of existence and give meaning to it, is transformed and becomes a mere sequence of discrete chronological units, perfectly countable and interchangeable. *Kairos* or the propitious moment for the Greeks, is here levelled and merged with the grey unravelling of *chronos*.

In the same overall picture, the relation between observer-researcher and object of observation is radically changed, and becomes positivist and neutral. The surprise is translated here into rhetorical questionings, not without a genuine pathos:

Is it ever possible to observe ourselves as an external, inanimate thing? Is it ever possible to hypothesize a supreme effort of the intelligence to pursue an understanding which then relieves us from thinking? Don't say it: they are metaphysical arguments! Once they were the themes of theodicy, when rationalism tried to reconcile human shortsightedness with divine omniscience. With the death of God, we men also inherited those questions of principle his untimely demise had not let him resolve.[36]

Here is a death more alive than the living. Here is an idea of science as absolute, timeless certainty, necessary and necessitating, which corresponds to the erroneous belief that

the only way of doing rational science is a tendential adjustment to the deductive forms of mathematics and Aristotelian logic. Underneath, there is a deceptive and deceiving relation with the public, as if history could be science only as a system of necessary propositions able to impose itself on all rational beings and on which agreement could be inevitable, beyond that of the techniques of argument.[37]

The everyday represents strongly the time of life in its existential connotation, distinguishing it from historical time and institutional time. Here, the limits of the conceptions of the everyday which relate it to, and exhaust its meaning in, simple repetitiveness become clear: in iteration, that is, and reproduction as instrument of order and social control. What is too easily forgotten is the revelatory and disruptive function of the everyday confronted with the great social reforms by decree, which seem to revolutionize the institutional fabric but do not manage to dent the quality of daily life.[38] Researchers have not always taken into account these basic disguises. The technical motivations of research and its logic have mostly won over the description and interpretation of the story and temporality of the witnesses.[39] Among contemporary historians, Fernand Braudel has seemed aware of the problem of synchronization, but his suggestions have certainly not resolved it. As against Marx, who stressed the relations of production, and Weber, who emphasized the importance of formal bureaucratic organizations, Braudel hinges his analyses on market relations and tends towards the construction of a "global history" in the precise sense that, rather than setting out institutional, structural typologies, relatively cutting them out of time, he aims at identifying a plurality of durations, and stresses the opposition between *le temps court*, the short time, and *la longue durée*, the long duration.

He thus distinguishes three levels in history: long periods of at least a century; phases of economic and social history of a generation—probably close to the sense of the "generation" of Ortega y Gasset, in *Aurora della ragione storica*; and the history of great events, history in the sense of traditional historiography. In Braudel the moment of the link between the three levels was missing, with the obvious result of several parallel histories which in turn are ignorant of, instead of facing, each other, intersecting and conditioning each other.

Again the everyday is reduced to its shadow, and the sleep-walking of the everyday mounts guard over the status quo in the name of custom or, as Weber would say, as the accredited representative of the "authority of the eternal yesterday." The apparently static, but really ecstatic and demonstrative function of the everyday has not been seen, the deep meaning of gestures repeated every day, the family realities, apparently without aura and importance, whereas they are fundamental and linked with the very springs of life. For this end, one needed the eye and voice of a poet, like Robert Walser in his "Conversation with a Button":

Dear little button, how much gratitude is owed you, by he whom for many years—more than seven, I believe—you have served with such loyalty, zeal and perseverance, and from whom, to the shame of all the oversight and forgetfulness with which he has sinned in your regard, you have never asked a crumb of praise. . . . That you give yourself no importance, that you are, or at least appear to be, all one with your life's mission, and feel wholly consecrated to the tacit discharge of that duty one may call an exquisitely scented rose, of a beauty itself almost an enigma, perfumed with a perfume wholly disinterested because it is only its destiny—is for me a reason for enchantment.[40]

What does this mean? A complete answer is difficult. To use a formula and in terms which may seem so abused as to be worn-out, I might say it means the retrieval and complete reacquisition of interiority, not as an evasion, but as a deepening. Iteration has mostly been seen and interpreted as the decisive factor of unreflecting self-realization and thus of stupefaction by the everyday. However, another interpretation is possible. The spiritual and real situation of this age awaits, indeed demands, this interpretation, radically alternative to the current one. In reality, iteration offers the opportunity for the deepening of *not* escaping from oneself, for learning to live with the problem. *In interiore homine stat veritas.* Here there emerges the question of the two truths: truth as precision, quantitatively measured and expressed, and truth as internal awareness and mastery of experience. The future of technically advanced societies depends on the practical and theoretical way of posing and resolving the tension that runs between these two basic conceptions of truth.

NOTES

1. Cf. the unpublished essay by Guy Oakes, "Weber in the South West German School: The Genesis of the Concept of the Historical Individual," contributed to the staff seminar of the New School for Social Research, New York, Spring 1985.

2. R. Calasso, *La rovina di Kasch* (Milan: Adelphi, 1983), p. 47.

3. P. Crespi, *Prete operaio* (Rome: Edizioni lavoro, 1985), p. 16.

4. For an impressive example see Georges Perec, *La vie mode d'emploi* (Paris: Hachette, 1978).

5. E. H. Carr, *Sei lezioni sulla storia* (Turin: Einaudi, 1966), p. 99. See too F. Diaz, *Storicismi e storicità* (Florence: Parenti, 1965).

6. P. Veyne, *Come si scrive la storia* (Rome-Bari: Laterza, 1973).

7. E. Garin, *Cronache ci filosofia italiana* (Rome-Bari: Laterza, 1956).

8. See the second appendix to the French translation of my *Histoire et histoires de vie* (Paris: Les Méridiens-Klincksieck, 1983), "Observations préliminaires sur le rapport entre histoire et sociologie à l'égard des histoires de vie," pp. 173–191.

9. For an authoritative contrary view see Lawrence Stone, "Il ritorno all narrazione: riflessioni su una vecchia nuova storia," *Comunitá* 35 (November 1981): 1–25.

10. Cf. G. Cotroneo, "I piani della storia," *Rivista di studi crociani* 3 (1975): p. 14.

11. B. Croce, *Pensiero politico e politica attuale* (Rome-Bari: Laterza, 1946).

12. Published by Laterza in 1981.

13. I. Mancini, in *L'Unitá*, 21.vii.1981.

14. W. Dilthey, *Critica della ragione storica* (Italian translation, Turin: Einaudi, 1954), p. 80 (my emphasis).

15. T. W. Adorno, *Note sulla letteratura* (Turin: Einaudi, 1963) vol. 1, p. 13.

16. See Gian Michele Tortelone, "Corporeita—Linee per una ricerca," *Rivista di teologia morale* 66 (April-June 1985): 39. "In bodies there appears the possible meaning of things, and only a *theology of pleasure* manages to grasp, perceive, the dynamics of the spirit which acts within life. Corporealness allows the discovery of a spiritual value in eroticism. Eroticism is that which, through bodies, expresses the depth of the beauty of life, confirms the transcendence of the flesh and materiality insofar as they are made live, inhabited by the presence of the spirit" (emphasis in original).

17. See "La sociologie en Italie," *Cahiers internationaux de sociologie* 78 (1985), and two editorials in *La critica sociologica*, 63 and 64, Autumn-Winter 1982–1983; 69, Spring 1984.

18. That in middling culture a certain positivistic and scientistic mentality should continue, it is no surprise and does not destroy the fact that social sciences had been wiped out from the Italian universities.

19. See especially *La sociologia come partecipazione* (Turin: Taylor, 1961); also *La piccola cittá*, especially chapter 2, "La ricerca sociologica come rapporto interpersonale."

20. R. Cavallaro, *Storie senza storia* (Roma: Centro Emigrazione, 1981) (emphasis in original).

21. G. Lutte, "A proposito di *Vite di periferia*," *La critica sociologica* 59 (Autumn 1981), p. 103.

22. Nuto Revelli, especially in *Mondo dei vinti*, has long emphasized this aspect of his work; as in *L'anello forte*, he refers to his
interest in the Italy of the poor peasant, by relating his basic experiences of the war, in January 1943, as an officer in the Alpini on
the Russian front. Here he discovered the fundamental convergence
between Italian and Russian peasants, destined for massacre, as his
experience of partisan warfare in the valleys of Cuneo confirmed.

23. For another *Autobiography of a Slave*, see that by Frederick
Douglas, ed. by Carole Beebe Tarantelli with a full bibliography rai-
sonnée by Alessandro Portelli (Rome: Savelli, 1978). Einaudi has announced the forthcoming study by Portelli of the city of Terni.

24. *La città come fenomeno di classe* (Milan: F. Angeli; Centro E.
Nathan Le "ricerche romane" di F. Ferrarotti, Rome).

25. For Oscar Lewis, whom I dealt with in Chapter 1 of *Vite di
barracati*, I refer to the first monograph, in America or Europe, dedicated to this typically multi-disciplinary anthropologist: L. Ferrarotti, *Oscar Lewis biografo della povertà* (Roma-Bari: Laterza, 1986).

26. F. Ferrarotti et al., *Studi e ricerche sul potere*, vol. 3 (Rome:
Ianua, 1980–1982).

27. *Biografia, storia, società*, (Naples: Liguori, 1985), pp. 29–33.

28. See, for example, A. Zucconi, *Autobiografia di un paese* (Milan:
Comuni, 1984).

29. See my *Dal documento alla testimonianza—l'uso della fotogra-
fia nelle scienze sociali* (Naples: Liguori, 1974). Perhaps because of
poor promotion, as regards sociologists, and with very few excep-
tions, my suggestion fell on deaf ears.

30. I take the formula in part from Philippe Lejeune, *Le pacte autobiographique* (Paris: Seuil, 1975). See too his *Je est un autre*, (Paris:
Seuil, 1980).

31. *Le pacte autobiographique*, p. 14.

32. Anna Riva, "Autobiografia e psicanalisi," in *Biografia, storia,
società*, p. 122.

33. Pietro Clemente, "Per l'edizione critica di testi biografici orali," *Fonti orali—Studi e ricerche* 4, no. 1 (1984): 22.

34. Ibid.

35. See the penetrating remarks in Cavallaro, *Storie senza storia*.

36. E. Melandri, "Introduzione" to A. Schutz, *La fenomenologia del
mondo sociale* (Bologna: Il Mulino, 1974), p. xvi.

37. G. Levi, "Introduzione" to F. Ramella, *Terra e telai* (Turin: Einaudi, 1985), p. vii.

38. For an initial approach to the problem see L. Balbo, "Il nostro
diritto quotidiano," *Rinascita* August 24, 1985, 31 pp. 6–7.

39. Cf. the remarks of Ch. Lalive d' Epinay, "Récit de vie et projet spécifique," in *Biografia, storia, societá*.

40. Robert Walser, *Vita di poeta* (Milan: Adelphi, 1985), pp. 122–123.

Annotated Bibliography

Albano, Gianfranco, and Sellari, Maricla. *Storie allo specchio* (*Stories in the mirror*). Turin: Eri, 1984.

The title relates to a TV program transmitted between 1978 and 1981, inspired by the idea of "giving a voice and a face to the 'hidden' protagonists of our reality," to the common people. The method adopted: that of examining the cases suggested after an initial TV announcement, followed by a preliminary meeting with those who had put themselves forward, and a judgment concerning the ability of the individuals to recount their own story in front of the camera. There were men and women, young and old; the subjects emerging: confrontation with institutions, problems concerning identity crisis or assertion, individual existential and social difficulty. Clearly in the movement from screen to page a series of visual elements that had enriched the stories was lost. The immediate impact on the viewer by way of the personal narrator can also be less effective in the written text, which could have used a commentary by the editors. This still remains a useful example of how TV can at times promote contributions of a remarkably high level of culture and information.

Anania, Francesca. "Biografia, storia e societa" ("Biography, history, and society"). *Italia contemporanea* no. 146, 147 (1982): 212–213.

The proceedings of the conference on this subject held in Rome in November 1981, attended by the historian Paul Thompson and the sociologists C. Lalive d'Epinay and Daniel Bertaux. Subjects discussed: the innovative potential in the field of historiography of the biographical method, methods of application to problems of social change, and of the use and interpretation of biographical materials.

Andreas-Salome, Lou. *Eintragungen. Letzte Jahre*. Frankfurt am Main: Insel Verlag, 1982.

This is the personal diary of the last years of an exceptional woman: the inspiration of Friedrich Nietzsche, companion of Rainer Maria Rilke for many years, and favorite disciple of Sigmund Freud. Her contemporaries especially found it hard to grasp the continuity of her interests, her underlying rationale, and above all the originality of her thought. This diary, halfway between the record of her everyday life in a mood of unguarded subjectivism, sometimes tormented, and the philosophical essay tackling the great questions—happiness, death, God—does justice to the author and persuasively makes the case for her independent spirit almost thirty years after her death in February 1937. Most immediately striking here is her suffering positiveness, succeeding despite her pain, awareness of death, and indeed her cosmic anguish. It is thus legitimate to argue that this posthumous work by Andreas-Salome, however subjective, really encapsulates the spirit of German culture from the end of the last century to the 1930s. However, this ought not to be so surprising, as the author grasped what so many modern, facile vulgarizers of great feelings struggle to see. She wrote: "Only the person who stays on their own ground can then be capable of being loved in a lasting way, as only this person, through their living self-sufficiency, can symbolize for another the potency of life. Everyone must sink their roots in their own soil, with no mutual dependency, so as to make themselves a World in the eyes of the person loved." Here, the paradox is penetratingly expressed of the distance which is necessary, even though it seems to deny it, to love. Here too lies the strength, the supreme assurance of Andreas-Salome, who can "nonchalantly mix life with death." There is at the same time a great disinterest in the self, the calm which watches over pure knowledge, which made Nietzsche think of the "cow in the meadow," peaceful, quiet, ruminating. "Infancy, or primitive humanity, because of its initially reduced individualism, preserves intact the ability of putting oneself in unison with all things, a kind of forgetfulness of self within the brutal instincts of egoism." It is marvellous to see here how, with one intuitive sweep, she manages to grasp the void hidden behind the endless philosophical diatribes on the subject-object relation: "Whoever has known the happiness and suffering of being created a self-conscious subject also knows the situation where, with a creative gesture, one *abolishes* the fatal, disturbing gap between subject and object" (emphasis in original). The book ends on the abolition of this gap by stressing the importance of what occurs in life beyond individual projects: "Human folly is not, however, the doing of men . . . but merely of that which happens in us in the brief moment of our life."

Proceedings of the Fifth International Conference on Oral History, *Il potere e la società* (*Power and society*), Barcelona, 29–31 March 1985.

This international meeting examined an extremely varied series of relations between power and the methods and contents of oral history and of the techniques of collecting life-histories. At the heart of the discussion were such subjects as the relation between the image and the written and spoken word. However, a more systematic attempt at theoretical and methodological reflection, which could make the comparison between very distant and at times seemingly incompatible experiences fruitful, was absent.

Barthes, Roland. *Il grado zero della scrittura* (*Writing degree zero*). Turin: Einaudi, 1982.

Beaujour, Michel, "Théorie et pratique de l'autoportrait contemporain: Edgar Morin et Roland Barthes," in Delhaz-Sarlet, C., and Catani, M., eds., *Individualisme et autobiographie en Occident*, in *Revue de l'Institute de Sociologie*, 1982, no. 1–2 (reprinted by the University of Brussels, 1983).

This discussion centers on the concept of the self-portrait as the account of an intellectual and spiritual formation, but also as a meta-discourse, a memoir "immanent to the text."

Bateson, Mary Catherine. *Con occhi di figlia. Ritratto di Margaret Mead e Gregory Bateson*, translated by Milan: Feltrinelli, 1985.

This is an intellectual biography, intelligently written and with deep affection and respect by a woman who, apart from being the daughter of Margaret Mead and Gregory Bateson, is a scholar who has contributed on the same level as her parents, given her interest in linguistics and anthropology. She recalls her "long hours spent as a child, on the edge of intense conversations," from which she was to obtain a cast of mental openness, which "made it clear why I never retreated before abstraction and abstract speculation." She remembers her parents' different rhythms, her mother's tireless activism, the puttings-off and pauses of Gregory. "With them, the private was projected on a wider screen, as too the knowledge acquired in distant places was integrated into the decisions of daily life." Endowed with a powerful organizing gift, sure of herself and her love, Margaret took on an increasingly dominant role, which resulted in the break with Gregory, who transferred on her his bitterness towards his own mother and interpreted Margaret's efforts as a "continuous attempt at domination and manipulation." Hence arose the concern of Margaret to suggest alternative models, to give her daughter freedom: "The models for almost all the choices I have made were there, in the network my mother created with the explicit intention that I could construct any kind of life at all from the materials available: a marriage with or without children, open or monogamous marriage, fleeting or lasting, housework or profession, solitude or ties, love for men or for women. . . . She put me in contact with a variety of persons who had made profoundly different choices and represented different ways of being human, of making a family life, different ways of being a woman." In this situation, the highest teaching was that of accepting the different and of prizing individuality. The portraits of Margaret Mead and Gregory Bateson are complex and unforgettable, since in all Mary Catherine's reconstruction there is an attempt to give meaning to their individual actions and their life overall. Margaret tends to characterize herself as a strong woman and tendentially open to the unknown, full of "indulgence" towards her own culture of origin, convinced that "immersion in a different cultural system and recognizing the difference does not mean disorder but produces models of harmony, is for the anthropologist the point of departure for their own penetrative powers." A woman of great, various loves (male and female), and of deep loyalties, Margaret had both the jealous sense of her own and others' independence ("she laid claim to these partings, her readiness to be abandoned like her ability to leave, traversing customs and waiting rooms without turning back, leaving me in my turn free to go towards worlds unknown to her"), and a strong desire for totality. Hence came the pain when this was put at risk, when she felt less understood and understandable (at the death of Ruth Benedict, with whom she had relations of intellectual understanding and deep love, and when her marriage with Bateson was in crisis), and when she was aware that there was no longer anyone who knew all her output, which included the global sense of her own life.

The figure of Gregory is different. His daughter records his decision to teach her natural history, his patience in doing simple experiments with her: "It seems to me that he devoted a great deal of application and invention in devising the paths of exploration along which he wanted to lead me, helping me at the same time to rediscover the pleasure of his company." She recalls her father's decision to take American citizenship, even with his basic alienation from that type of culture: "He saw the whole system as so basically disconnected as to be useless, and so within the culture he took up a position of extraneousness, and did not bother to appreciate or protect its forms." Convinced of the "incongruity of any rivalry or jealousy," Gregory consistently applied these convictions, accepting the determining presence of Ruth Benedict in life with Margaret. He became interested in psychiatry, and his being in analysis and rebellion against Margaret ended "in an analysis of the models of communication in families of schizophrenics, and mainly in this context, the role of the mother." Love for the natural sciences was translated into a search for regularities and discords, of "indications for the formulation of models." Margaret was convinced that the problems could be resolved: Bateson was not, as his basic attitude was marked by a strong pessimism, abandoned only in the last years of his life. So, in 1967, he was to organize study seminars and "with the choice, abandoned an attitude which went back to wartime, when distrust of the possibility of a personal contribution and disgust with applied sociology had contributed to his depression."

His daughter remembers being called on, when Gregory's imminent death was feared, to write a book with him: an act of love and recognition of intellectual differences more important than any other, typical of persons whose life is spent in research and the weaving of meanings.

Bertaux, D., ed. *Biography and Society: The Life History Approach in the Social Sciences.* London: Sage, 1981.

This volume contains some of the contributions from well-known scholars at the Ninth World Congress of Sociology (Uppsala, August 1978). Among them, we note that of F. Ferrarotti, arguing for the conceptual and operational autonomy

of the biographical method, perceiving in it heuristic possibilities, which are presented as a new *Methodenstreit* (for example, "On the Autonomy of the Biographical Method," pp. 19–
27), and that of M. Kohli. The latter sees in biographies the
itineraries of the everyday as followed by a subject reacting
psychically and socially with the group. In addition, stimulating contributions from P. Thompson ("Life Histories and the
Analysis of Social Change"), J. Synge ("Cohort Analysis in the
Planning and Interpretation of Research Using Life History"),
and N. Gagnon ("On the Analysis of Life Accounts") should be
remembered.

Bertaux, Daniel, and Kohli, Martin. "The Life Story Approach—A
Continental View," in *Annual Review of Sociology* no. 10 (1984):
215–237.

The authors sketch an overview of the bibliography of the
uses and formulations regarding the biographic approach in
classical as well as more recent sociology; they put forward
their interpretation of the biographic method as a possible new
way of studying old problems, such as social mobility, emigration, and marginality. Bertaux in particular stresses the state
of research in Italy and France.

Bertelli, Paola O. "Un convegno du 'storie orali' " ("A Conference on
'Oral Histories' "). *La critica sociologica* no. 73 (1985): 114–
117.

The starting point is the fifth conference on oral history held
at Barcelona in March 1985, concentrating on the subject of
power. In fact, rather than a summary of the proceedings, there
are reflections on the "oral method," and on the need to refine
techniques and methodology so as to avoid the risk of a kind
of "political archaeology," or "militant research."

———. "Da tanti canti furon tanti pianti" ("From Many Songs Came
Many Laments"). *La critica sociologica* no. 68 (1983–1984): 81–
156.

The account of a woman who moved to Rome from Rocca di
Fondi, ending up eventually living in Magliana Nuova. Bertelli introduces the transcription of Rita's stories recalling the
most important moments, and sketching the outlines "of a
mentality which appears as a combination of persistent residues of a familial-peasant world and of new acquisitions rest-
ing on experience," elements which must be grasped in their
interaction. The testimony goes beyond the theme of poverty,
the framework in which initially it had first been collected.

————. "Fra storia e fonti orali" ("Between History and Oral Sources"). *La critica sociologica* no. 66 (1983): 148–150.

The account of the second national meeting on oral history held at Terni, April 1983, with the backing also of *Fonti orali: studi e ricerche,* and *Giorne cantati.* There was discussion of the backgrounds of research, orality and writing, interpretation and analysis of the biographic document, and of the presentation and use of oral sources. Bertelli records the chief positions appearing, and the current polemics.

"Biographie et societé," in *Bulletin de liaison du groupe de travail sur l'approche biographique en sciences sociales* no. 1 (1983) (special number).

Published by the foundation Maison des Sciences de l'Homme (54, Boulevard Raspail, 75270 Paris Cedex 06, France), this is the first of a series providing news about the activity of scholars working on the use of life histories in the social sciences, but in addition reports on the main studies in progress, with summaries, and the latest publications.

Blalock, H. *L'analisi causale in sociologia.* Padua: Marsilio, 1967.

Bravo, Anna; Passerini, Luisa; and Piccone Stella, Simonetta. "Modi di raccontarsi e forme di identitá nelle storie di vita" ("Modes of Giving Account of Oneself and Forms of Identity in Life Histories"). *Memoria* no. 8 (1983): 101–113.

A round table at which the dialogue between the three scholars, concerned with women's and feminist problematics, puts forward the biographic method as that closest to a sensibility and cultural heritage where "recounting—giving an account" and the relation with the female have a determinant role.

Brochier, Hubert. "Psychanalyse et désire d'autobiographie," in Delhez-Sarlet, C., and Catani, M., eds. *Individualisme et autobiographie en Occident,* pp. 177–185.

The author distinguishes between the autobiographic and the analytic method, over and above the superficial similarities. Autobiography "leads to setting up a monument, to painting itself standing in a historic pose, taking advantage of the occasion to settle certain accounts." Analysis, on the contrary, is based on the sternest sincerity with oneself and the interlocutor.

Burgos Debray, Elizabeth. *Me llamo Rigoberta Menchú (I Am Rigoberta Menchú).* Havana: Ediciones Casa de las Americas, 1983.

Rigoberta Menchú is a young Indian woman, belonging to

one of the twenty-two Guatemalan ethnic groups, from the El Quiche Department in the northeast. As Burgos Debray warns, she expresses herself in Spanish, a language she learned only three years ago, but still (in the author's view) this is an exemplary testimony "because it embodies the life of all Indians of the American Continent": the cultural discrimination she has suffered is the same as that of other Indians, as are the episodes of genocide. Rigoberta has "learnt the idiom of the oppressors to turn it against them": respecting her story, the text records her testimony, expressed directly, often in faulty Spanish, especially as regards verbs and prepositions. And this is a precise choice by the author, an anthologist. The text begins with a section on the family and birth ceremonies, follows with a description of conditions and types of work, struggles for land, the incarceration of her father, the torture and death of a brother, Rigoberta's decision to learn Spanish, and the march of the peasants on the capital. It continues with the account of the protagonist's life while being pursued by the army, her hiding in a convent, and her exile. In an appendix there is a series of manifestoes and newsheets from the National Committee of Union Unity, and a useful glossary with the meanings of idiomatic expressions appearing in the text.

Camargo, Aspasia. *The Intellectual and Politics: Meeting Alonso Arinos*. Rio de Janeiro: Editora Don Quixote, 1984.

———. *Northwest and Politics: Meeting José Americo de Almeida*. Rio de Janeiro: Nova Fronteira, 1984.

———. "The Uses of Oral and Life-History." *Dados*, 1984.

This is a special number devoted to life-histories, which also includes a series of lectures and contributions presented at the Centro de Pesquisa e Documentacao de Historia Contemporanea do Brasil, the Getulio Vargas Foundation, with the support of the Department of Anthropology. Among the subjects examined are the relations between oral history and rural studies (Ester Iglesias) the problems of exile from the women's viewpoint (Valentina da Rocha Lima and Lucia Hipolito), and the reconstruction of the conservative party in Brazil, by way of life-histories.

Campelli, Enzo. "Approccio biografico e inferenza scientifica" ("The Biographic Approach and Scientific Inference"). *Sociologia e ricerca sociale* no. 9, 3 (1982): 71–94.

In this contribution the biographic method is described as a "methodological infatuation"; it speaks of the "apparent facil-

ity of the work of collection and analysis it seems to require,"
with a subsequent " 'naturalistic' reappropriation of the role
of researcher by individuals and groups, also in competition if
not antagonism as regards those who have this role profes-
sionally (or academically)." Again, there is talk of a "political,
almost automatically progressive, stamp." It is recognized that
this method encourages research on an interdisciplinary basis;
it talks of a need for lessening overly strict "disciplinary defi-
nitions." However, according to the author, these demands run
the risk of ending in a "relative devaluing of sociology as a
specific discipline," provided with rules and binding procedures, in a confusion between sociology as a disciplinary "hard
core" and a generic sensitivity to social events and behavior—
elements that in Italian culture are a disappearing trick as
regards a basic ostracism. According to Campelli, this method
is accompanied by the negation of any organizational demand
on the researcher's part, the "refusal of analysis," and the simple presentation of the material (which, possibly, is collected
and organized by parthenogenesis): again, a "pretended humility by the researcher," in his view, "crosses over into methodological opportunism": too much devaluation, unsupported
sharpness, which to some extent raises doubts about itself and
makes one think of a neophyte's excess of zeal regarding
quantitative methods.

Campelli, Enzo; Cavallaro, Renato; Cipriani, Roberto; Padiglione,
Vincenzo; and Pozzi, Enrico. "Histoires de vie et groupes pri-
maires: une méthodologie pour l'analyse du phénomène reli-
gieux," *Actes de la xvi-ème CISR*. Lausanne, 1981, pp. 411–
423.

———. "Religione e storie di vita familiare" ("Religion and Family
Life Histories"). *Idoc internazionale* no. 2, 3 (1983): 26–30.

Canetti, Elias. *Il gioco degli occhi. Storia di una vita (1931–37)*. Milan:
Adelphi, 1985.

The third volume of Canetti's biography, Nobel prizewinner
for literature, the well-known author of *Crowds and Power*,
opens where *Il frutto del fuoco* left off. *Storia di una vita 1921–
1931*, with the description of his state of mind at the time of
the ending of *Auto da fé*, states *"Kant prende fuoco*—this was
then the title of the novel—had made a desert inside me. The
fire which destroyed the books was something I could not for-
give myself for. . . . During the writing of the book, Kant had
been so maltreated and I had been so tortured by repressing

every feeling of compassion towards him, by not leaving the slightest trace of compassion, that from the author's viewpoint putting an end to his existence was rather a liberation."

In this biography we meet famous and unknown people, such as Hermann Broch and Anna Mahler, daughter of the famous composer, whom Canetti loved deeply, and the sculptor Fritz Wotruba, Dr. Sonne, Ernst Bloch and many others. We encounter Viennese cafes where people talk, quarrel and sing, where the "discord of voices" arises, where "smoke and uproar were thrown in your face like dishrags" and there was no free seat to be found. We meet the lanes and inns of Grinzing, where at a certain hour "the real citizens of the place came onto the scene," "characters who in their strangeness and originality surpassed all the expectations of those who frequented the popular hostelries or the inns with greater pretensions." We also meet, now at the point of death, Canetti's mother, a fascinating woman of exceptional intelligence, a dominating figure in the first autobiographical volume, *La lingua salvata*. We meet Thomas Mann, but above all we meet Musil. Here Canetti presents a picture of the author of *The Man without Qualities* it is hard to forget: "Musil—without much appearing to—was always ready for battle, ready for defense and attack. His attitude was his security. . . . He traced boundaries between everything, as also within himself. He distrusted gatherings and friendships, effusions and exaggerations. He was a solid state man, and kept away from liquids and gases. . . . He never took part in general conversations, and if he found himself among the usual chatterers, which in Vienna it was impossible to avoid, he retreated into his shell and stayed silent." Canetti recalls some characteristic features, some idiosyncrasies: "He withdrew from undesired contacts. He wanted to stay master of his own body. I believe he never volunteered a handshake." He recalls "the competitive element in him," and says he is convinced "he knew his own value, and at least on this crucial issue was never touched by doubts, then or later. The few who were convinced of this were for him never convinced enough." In fact they longed to make comparisons with Broch or even James Joyce. Canetti recalls two difficult moments in their acquaintanceship. Once, when Canetti retold to Musil his own encounter with Joyce, "He showed signs of impatience: 'And did you have a good opinion of him?' he asked, and I could call myself fortunate if he changed the subject from

Joyce and did not leave me in the lurch." A second time, Musil
was congratulating Canetti over the publication of his novel:
"They were words which made me lose my head. . . . I was
drunk and confused, I must have been *very* confused, or how
else could I have committed the most dreadful of gaffes? I heard
him out, and then said at once 'And just imagine, I've even
had a long letter from Thomas Mann!' Musil changed like
lightning, as if he had retreated into himself with a bond, his
face turned grey and he was inside his shell. 'Ah yes,' he said.
He half gave me his hand, so I could only shake the fingers
and turned away sharply. So I was dismissed. This was a definitive dismissal. Musil was a master in imposing distances,
and had long practise in that art: if he rejected a person, he
rejected them for ever. . . . He never again let himself be
drawn into conversation with me."

Carey, James W. "Harold Adams Innis and Marshall McLuhan." *The
Antioch Review* 17, no. 1 (Spring 1967).

———. "The Mythos of the Electronic Revolution." *The American
Scholar* 39, no. 2 (Spring 1970).

Carey, James W., and John Quirk. "Canadian Communication Theory: Extensions and Evasions of Harold Innis." *The American
Scholar* 39, no. 3 (Summer 1970).

Carlotti, Anna Lisa. *Storia psicologia psicanalisi (History, psychology, psychoanalysis)*. Milan: Angeli, 1984.

A book of great clarity in which the basic convergences in
the human sciences are illuminated.

Catani, Maurizio. "Approccio biografico, formazione o autoforma-
zione" ("Biographical Approach, Formation and Self-Formation"). *La critica sociologica* no. 71, 72 (1984–1985); 153–160.

Catani presents the debate opened up around some of Ferrarotti's contributions at Paris Dauphine, at the invitation of
Guy Jobert, director of "Education permanente," stressing the
relations with ethnography, the theoretical relation between
the general and the particular, and the problems of formation
and self-formation.

———. "De l'enseignement centre sur l'ecoute et l'expression de soi
a l'approche biographique orale," in *Education permanente* no.
72, 73 (1984): 97–119.

The author presents a typology of "life stories" where the
"history of social life" is brought out positively, in relation to
its characteristics of chorality and ritualized transmission of
the social.

————. "Gli emigranti. Dai valori localistici alla planetarizzazione dell'individualismo occidentale" ("The Emigrants: From Localist Values to the Planetarization of Western Individualism"). *La ricerca folclorica* no. 7 (1983): 53–62.

————. "L'histoire de vie sociale de Tante Suzanne est un échange oral ritualisé." In Delhez-Sarlet, C., and Catani, M. *Individualisme et autobiographie en Occident*, pp. 63–72.

The author presents his research, devoted for many years to gathering a single social life-history, bringing out the relation established between observer and observed in a defined ethnological framework, as one of "ritualized symbolic exchange," where the "word" circulates between two persons, creating a "symbolic totality."

Catani, Maurizio, and Berthelier, Robert. "La psicopatologia del trapianto: considerazioni relative al caso di migranti, dei loro figli e all'impossibile ritorno dei figli nei paesi dei genitori" ("The Psychopathology of Transplant: Considerations on the Case of Emigrants, Their Children, and the Impossible Return of the Children to the Countries of Their Parents). *La critica sociologica* no. 60 (1981–1982): 6–15.

The discussion of these subjects and problems is accompanied by a series of direct testimonies supporting the theoretical viewpoint.

Catani, Maurizio, and Mazé, Suzanne. *Tante Suzanne. Une histoire de vie sociale.* Paris: Librairie des Méridiens, 1982.

This is the story of a woman, or, as the subtitle puts it, 'the story of the social life and becoming of a woman' who was first Mayenne milliner at the time of the World War I, afterwards the wife of a Paris watchmaker, mother of two children, and owner of a garden in the famous suburb, who never denied her origins. In a very dense methodological section, Catani compares the historical process of individuation characteristic of the West, the emergence of the Ego and the production of a life story. This leads him to propose a typology of products of the biographical approach, which goes from "accounts of practices limited in time" to the "autobiography . . . in which the use of writing eliminates the constitutive presence of the listener." The history of social life is the fifth stage: it is defined as an "account which involves the comparison and evaluation of events by a narrator who as such includes the function of values." This is the case of Suzanne Mazé's account.

Cavallaro, Renato. "L'emigrazione fra storia e memoria." In *La critica sociologica* no. 74 (1985): 136–138.

This is a precise summary of the conference on "Integration and cultural identity of immigrants in Argentina," held in Buenos Aires in August 1985, where room was given to oral and written sources for the study of immigration.

———. "L'individuo e il gruppo. Riflessioni sul metodo biografico." *Sociologia* no. 1 (1981): 49–68.

A double methodological suggestion, on the one hand tending to reduce the life history to a problematic historical document in which the concept of social action and that of linguistic intersubjectivity are engraved; and on the other, it is proposed to have recourse to the concepts of social time and space (sociological chronotope) to understand the relation between individual and social group. The role of participant observation is basic.

———. "Mein Vater, mio padre, mon pere: socioanalisi della figura paterna in testimonianze autobiografiche di figli di lavoratori italiani emigrati" ("Socio-analysis of the Father Figure in Autobiographical Testimonies by Sons of Italian Emigrants"). *Dossier Europa-Emigrazione* no. 6–7 (1984): 6–13.

———. "La memoria biografica" ("Biographical memory"). *Estudios Migratorios Latino Americanos* no. 1 (1986): 106–129.

This concerns the importance of the biographical method in the study of problems such as emigration. A special section is devoted to the techniques of reporting and setting up the research: for example, a distinction is made between individual, group, and cross-linked biographies (the latter are based on experimental transfers of some subjects into several groups), and a guide to discussion is presented.

———. *Storie senza storia. Indagine sull'emigrazione calabrese in Gran Bretagna* (*Stories without History: Inquiry into Calabrian Immigration in Great Britain*). Rome: Centro Studi Emigrazione, 1981.

The themes of orality and writing and the dominant use of linguistic analysis are the basis of this study concerning some examples of Calabrian immigrants to Bedford. The various ways in which time is experienced are examined (narrative time and social times, social experience of time, free time and the family, festive time in its deployment regarding ceremonies and rituals) and space (social space, industrial space, "happy" space connected with the theme of the home, space in life lived in the city and at home), social groups, and daily life. The book concentrates especially on some examples of morphosyntax, as, for example, the type of logical agreement, clauses, the pronoun system and redundancy, analogic comparison, the use of adjectives instead of adverbs, etc. The stories follow.

Celli, Angelo. *Odissea e biografia di Angelo Celli e tutta la sua famiglia,* ed. CO.IL.S.E., Novafeltria 1986.

The subtitle is *Per una storia dell'alta Valmarecchia nella seconda metá dell'Ottocento.* The testimony of Angelo Celli is expanded by notes and comments by collaborators at the Centro culturale C. M. Alta Valmarecchia and accompanied by fine photographs of people and places of the time. The methodological notes by Vittorio Dini that end the book are very instructive.

Cipriani, Roberto. "Il caso di Valle Aurelia." *La critica sociologica* no. 63–64 (1982–1983): 93–170.

This involves a reading of biographical materials collected in the area of Valle Aurelia, with special attention to the subject of poverty.

———. *Il Cristo rosso. Riti e simboli, religione e politica nella cultura popolare (The Red Christ: Rites, Symbols, Religion and Politics in Popular Culture).* Rome: Ianua, 1985.

———. "Povertá urbana e marginalitá: il ruolo della Chiesa" ("Urban Poverty and Marginality: The Role of the Church"). *La critica sociologica* no. 57–58 (1981): 133–142.

———. "Riti e simboli della settimana santa in Capitanata; il Cristo rosso in Cerignola." *Rappresentazioni arcaiche della tradizione popolare.* Viterbo: Centro di Studi sul teatro medioevale e rinascimentale, 1982.

———. "Le storie di vita e il caso italiano" ("Life-histories and the Italian Case"). *La critica sociologica* no. 63–64 (1982–1983): 244–245.

The interpretative lines of the paper presented at Mexico City (Tenth ISA Congress) by Maria I. Macioti, concerning Italy, are given. This gathers togethers the main lines of interpretation emerging from research and contributions based on the biographical method, with special emphasis on sociology and cultural anthropology.

———. "Review of R. Cavallaro, *Storie senza storia." Studium* no. 6 (1982): 776–777.

Cipriani, Roberto; Pozzi, Enrico; and Corrado, Consuelo. "Histoires de vie familiale dans un contexte urbain." *Cahiers internationaux de sociologie* no. 79 (1985): 253–262.

Citarella, Filippo. *Las sociologia come scienza del singolare, Note sul metodo biografico (Sociology as Science of the Singular: Notes on the Biographical Method.* Preface by F. Ferrarotti. Palermo: Mazzone, 1983.

Clapier-Valladon, Simone; Poirier, Jean; and Raybaut, Pierre. *Les récits de vie. Théorie et pratique.* Paris: PUF, 1983.

———. "La collecte du récit biographique." *Education permanente,* no. 72–73 (1984): 65–74.

The authors analyze the nature and techniques of the *entretien,* the discussion at the center of the relation between observer and the observed, interviewer and interviewee. More exactly, this relation appears similar to that of literary origin, between narrator and narrated, in a kind of Socratic interrogation and social maieutics.

Contini, Giovanni. "Fonti orali e fonti scritti: un confronto." *Classe* no. 18 (1980): 285–328.

Coste, Didier. "Autobiographie et auto-analyse, matrices du texte littéraire." In Delhez-Sarlet, C., and Catani, M. *Individualisme et autobiographie en Occident,* pp. 249–264.

The author proposes a typification able to take account of the "deep structure of an intimate text": autobiography, self-analysis, and "self-perspectives" coexist and, in the conflict, are presented as a "linguistic consciousness" of the text.

Crespi, Pietro. "Narrazione e ascolto. Aspetti e problemi dell' approccio orale in sociologia" ("Narration and Listening, Aspects and Problems of the Oral Approach in Sociology"). *La critica sociologica* no. 70 (1984): 41–52.

Attention is focused on the importance of language, and the instruments of oral communication, whose use "implies the recognition that situations, processes and individual facts involve a universe of objectives and references associated with the categorical language of thought, methods of explanation, stereotypes and value systems." In Crespi's version, social memory and historical memory coincide: "they are organized memory," where "one may embrace the multiple aspects of a cultural picture grasped as a whole"; expressed in orality, it sees in the concrete "complex temporal structures which make the traditional itineraries of systems of inference problematic, so that in this instance they seem to float on the waters of an unassailable objectivity." In this context, where the sugges-

tiveness of the discussion is never divorced from a firm scientific rigor, one of the protagonists is silence, which "plays an
active role in the linkages of the narrative dialogue, [which]
is more often subject than object, and presents in specific contexts its own structural originality."

──────. *Prete operaio (Worker Priest)*. Rome: Edizioni Lavoro, 1985.
By way of autobiographical testimony of exceptional immediacy, the author reconstructs lives and itineraries of thought
that reach the depths of the maturing of vocations and life
projects as regards a situation—that of the worker priest in
Italy—which is still an open problem and also a scandal for
official Italian society. Here the biographical approach shows
all its richness and the validity of its support it can give today
to research in the human sciences.

D'Amato, Marina. "Biografia, storia e societá: un convegno multidis-
ciplinare." *La critica sociologica* no. 59 (1981): 142–146.

De Bernart, Maura. "I documenti personali. 'Buona ricerca' e 'men-
talitá metodologica' americana nelle scienze sociali (1938–
1945)." *Sociologia* 16, no. 1 (1982): 67–98.
A discussion of the debate in the Social Science Research
Council between 1938 and 1945 in the United States. In this
long, polemical debate so-called "good" research based on so-
phisticated quantitative methods was counterposed to sociological research based on personal documents.

──────. "L'uso delle autobiografie nell'analisi sociologica della de-
viana giovanile urbana." *Sociologia urbana e rurale* 2, no. 5
(1981): 225–246.
A study in deviance carried out in Rome betwen 1975 and
1976, using life-histories. The research, carried out in two Roman *borgate*, uses autobiography as an instrument capable of
bringing out the basic elements of that particular reading of
reality common to young deviants. The difficulty of analyzing
the histories must be stressed while the remarkable potential
of the method remains.

Delhez-Sarlet, Claudette, and Catani, Maurizio, eds. *Individualisme
et autobiographie en Occident*. Brussels: Editions de l'Université
de Bruxelles, 1983.
In this international seminar, organized by the Centre Cul-
turel International de Cerisy-La-Salle, 10–20 July 1979, the
theme of the rise of the Ego as a phenomenon typical of Western society was faced in an interdisciplinary way, with contributions ranging from ethnology to sociology, psychoanalysis,

law, and literature. The main reference point is historical
analysis, which seeks to identify the times and forms wherein
the autobiographical thrust is manifested from early Christianity to today.

Denzin, Norman K. "Interpreting the Lives of Ordinary People: Hei-
degger, Sartre and Faulkner." *Dados. Revista de Ciencias So-
ciais* (1984) (*Life Histories/Histoires de vie*, 1, 1985).

———. "On Interpreting an Interpretation." *American Journal of
Sociology* 89, no. 6 (1984): 1426–1433.

———. *On understanding emotion.* San Francisco: Jossey-Bass, 1984.

———. "Reinterpreting the Polish peasant." In Dulczewski, Zyg-
munt, eds. *Florian Znaniecki.* Warsaw: forthcoming.

Didier, Beatrice. *Stendhal autobiographique.* Paris: Presses Univer-
sitaires de France, 1983.

The author explores the ways whereby Stendhal arrived at
La vie de Henry Brulard, and stresses the difference between
autobiography and biography: "In autobiography the author
commits himself to the reader," promising him the story of *his*
life, not that of another.

Dupas, Jean Claude. "Dire 'je' en Angleterre au xvii siècle. Excen-
trations et contradictions." In Delhez-Sarlet, pp. 115–126.

The importance of spiritual autobiography in the emergence
of bourgeois self-consciousness and the concept of the individual.

Farge, Arlette. *La vie fragile, violence, pouvoirs et solidarités à Paris
au dix-huitième siecle.* Paris: Nachette, 1986.

A documentary reconstruction of daily life in Paris in the
eighteenth century. The sources are secondary archival ones,
especially from police and judicial archives. No wonder, then,
that the central figure of the picture is that of the district police commissioner, who deals with the problems and quarrels
and conflicts of the families in the neighborhood. The function,
and hence the social position, of the police inspector is, on the
other hand, different. The "social space" of the district is first
examined, then the book moves on to the masses of the urban
setting in all its variety.

Ferrarotti, Franco. "Les biographies comme instrument analytique
et interprétatif." *Cahiers Internationaux de Sociologie* no. 69
(1980): 227–248.

Starting from the concept that social marginality linked to
poverty is above all a structural situation, the author carefully examines and criticizes Oscar Lewis's thought and iden-

tifies its conceptual weaknesses. Centered on the family, Lewis's study basically tends to give slight consideration to class relations and the mechanisms that cause them. On the other hand, one must use a methodology that takes life histories as basic instruments for understanding and broadening the far-reaching dynamics of the emargination found in large metropolitan ghettoes.

―――. "Biography and the Social Sciences." *Social Research* 50, no. 1 (1983): 57–80.

―――. *Cinque scenari per il Duemila* (English translation: *Five Scenarios for the Year 2000*, Westport, CT: Greenwood, 1986).

―――. *Giovanni e droga*. Naples: Liguori, 1976.

―――. "Una metodologia sociologica come tecnica dell'ascolto" ("A Sociological Methodology as a Technique for Listening"). *La critica sociologica* no. 56 (1980–1981): 17–46.

―――. "On the autonomy of the biographical method." In Bertaux, Daniel, ed., pp. 19–27.

―――. *Vite di baraccati*. Naples: Liguori, 1973.

―――. *Vite di periferia (Lives on the periphery)*. Milan: Mondadori, 1981.

Materials gathered in the areas of Magliana Nuova and Valle Aurelia in Rome are presented; testimonies, in direct form, transcribed orthophonically, follow a structural picture of the areas. In them an account of the environment and methods of discussion is given, as are descriptions of the disturbances encountered. There are brief introductions to the individual conversations, which at times are hard to read because the modes of oral language (pauses, slowness in reaching the point, frequent repetition, linguistic difficulties, etc.) are preserved as far as possible.

Ferrarotti, Franco; Magli, Ida; Cagnetta, Franco; and Lutte, Gerard. "A proposito di vite di periferia." *La critica sociologica* no. 59 (1981): 66–83.

This involves contributions to the presentation of *Vite di periferia* at the Paesi Nuovi bookshop in Rome. Ida Magli stresses attention given to the group rather than the individual and the type of language of the protagonists of these lives. Franco Cagnetta, the famous author of *Banditi a Orgosolo*, intervenes polemically against a certain voluntarism he discerns in Lutte and Magli, discusses the idea of wanting to change the *borgate* of Rome and Paris when possible alternative forms are not requested or suggested by those interviewed, and declares himself wholly in disagreement with Pasolini and a psychologistic approach to the problem. Lutte says he is quite convinced of the interest of the materials of the kind suggested in the text in producing greater awareness in people, and in relation to a possible social change. Finally, Ferrarotti concludes, stressing the need for providing the context of biographical materials, as well as a process of interaction that alone can bring out its full scientific productivity.

Ferrarotti, Laura. "Storie orali per una storia di Portorico." *La critica sociologica* no. 74 (1985): 63–65.

An account is given of the activities of the Center for Puerto Rican studies through an interview with Rina Ben Mayor of Hunter College, NY.

———. *Oscar Lewis biografo della povertá*. Rome-Bari: Laterza, 1986.

This is the first monograph devoted to the American scholar, anthropologist by training, and pupil of Ruth Benedict, to whom we owe some highly interesting and successful books, as *La Vida*, *The Children of Sanchez*, and *Pedro Martinez*, and the definition of the concept of the "culture of poverty." The book places him in the context of American anthropology, examines his work and methods, concentrating especially on *La Vida* and the relations between Lewis and literature. Lewis's biography uses archival sources as well as published works. The analysis of how dialogic discourse is changed, in the passage from orality to writing, into analogic discourse, is important.

Gadamer, H. G. *Truth and Method*. Edited and translated by Garrett Barden and John Cumming. New York: Seabury Press, 1975.

Gagnon, Nicole. "Données autobiographiques et praxis culturelle," *Cahiers internationaux de sociologie* no. 69 (1980): 291–304.

A contribution on biography conceived of as the expression of individual identity as privileged material of "living culture," showing a strong, mature critical spirit.

Gentili, Bruno. *Poesia e pubblico nella Grecia antica*. Rome-Bari: Laterza, 1984.

———. "Oralitá e cultura arcaica" ("Orality and Archaic Culture"). *La critica sociologica* no. 68 (1983–1984): 16–31.

The author stresses the decidedly pragmatic character of Greek poetry, an expression to be understood "in the sense of a close connection with social and political reality, and with the concrete action of the individuals in the collectivity," of basic links with oral communication and music. For a poetry to be defined as oral, in his view, there must exist the conditions of orality of composition, communication, and transmission: these may exist simultaneously or separately. The art of memory, in Gentili's version, has always been "one of the basic instruments for the preservation of data and the ideas which formed the framework of a cultural tradition," the foundation of Greek culture; distinction should be made between "the memory of poetic themes and formulas and the mechanical memory of texts rigidly transmitted word by word." In this perspective the question of Homer should also be examined.

Gentili, Bruno, and Cerri, G. *Storia e biografia nel pensiero greco.* Rome-Bari: Laterza, 1983.

Giddens, Anthony. *New Rules of Sociological Method.* London: Blackwell, 1978.

Graff, Harvey J. "Reflections on the History of Literacy: Overview, Critique and Proposals." *Humanities in Society* no. 4 (1981): 303–333.

———. "Literacy and Social Developments in North America: On Ideology and History." In *Aspects of literacy in the eighteenth and nineteenth centuries,* ed. W. B. Stephens. Leeds: Museum of the History of Education, U. of Leeds, 1983, pp. 82–97, 103–106.

———. "On literacy in the Renaissance: Overview and Reflections." *History of Education* no. 12 (1983): 69–85.

———. "The History of Literacy: Toward the Third Generation." *Interchange* no. 17 (1986).

Guglielminetti, Marziano. "L'autobiographie en Italie xiv et xvii siècles." In Delhez-Sarlet, pp. 101–114.

On the importance of religious literature, especially autobiographical, but also of the accounts of merchant families, in the development of individual consciousness in the Renaissance middle classes.

———. *Memoria e scrittura.* Turin: Einaudi, 1977.

A most interesting excursus on the autobiographical method in Dante and Cellini, passing through Petrarch, Boccaccio, and the records and memoirs of writer-merchants and politicans to arrive at Cellini's *Life* and the memoirs of the artists. Openly polemical with Philippe Lejeune, who in *Le pacte autobiographique* had shown his slight acquaintance of Italian autobiographers (as also of Spanish and Russian ones), not even cited in the still ample bibliography, the author remarks that "not always, and in any case not necessarily, does the medieval or Renaissance reader of autobiography belong to the public of those who enjoy other literary genres of the age. It may even not exist for long periods, and the macroscopic case is suggested by Cellini's *Vita*, published posthumously, certainly not for reasons of chance; or else it may challenge a social nucleus, the family, connected by ties of kinship with the writer (this is the case of the merchant memoir). To imagine thus that value judgment on the autobiographical product were already possible for the reader of the time "has almost no basis, at least for many texts." Of special interest is the exploration of the origins of autobiography, in which a large part is naturally given to St. Augustine's *Confessions*, which, moreover, "places at the root of the discussion knowledge of God. It can only guarantee him knowledge of himself, but with a bargain, that by writing he entrusts everything to the power of evocation and construction of memory, the only power able to take man away from the strength of attraction of material life." However, on the other hand, the "function of memory is wholly vicarious as regards the preliminary and constraining one of ethical and ascetic judgment." Time is thus not chronologically transcribable, but only "spiritually to be listened to," in that in its essence lies the same rhythm of the creature existence of man. Hence, the function of memory, which does not consist in recalling things to life, things now irrevocably past and perished, is rather the "words which have fixed the image of those things in the mind." After the *Confessions*, this supreme identity between memory and *verba*, memory and writing, Guglielminetti argues—an identity guaranteed by God and His changeless presence—no longer holds up, and breaks down so that Raterius and Abelard, representative exponents of the autobiographical genre in the centuries preceding the rise of popular literature "reject both structuring the tale in time and submitting it to the sifting process of the divine presence." In fact, between the fifth and thirteenth centuries, autobiographical writing distances itself from the Augustinian model. The writer's conclusion is that "from that distant and now almost vanished prototype there is above all a crisis in the inventive and supporting function of memory, according to a trend already existing in the slender but existing autobiographical tradition of medieval Latin literature. This tendency, with the rise and assertion of the literatures in the vulgar tongue, was not fought in Italy: rather, the more or less conscious attempt to replace Augustine with Francesco, instead of holding it in, ended by preserving its line of march."

Henige, David. *Oral Historiography*. London: Longman, 1982.

Hernandez, Francesco. *L'identidad nacional en Cataluna*. Barcelona: Vicens Vives, 1983.

"Les histoires de vie." *Education permanente* no. 72–73 (1984).

"Histoires de vie et vie sociale." Special number of *Cahiers internationaux de sociologie* no. 69 (1980).

    This number contains a series of essays placing the subject on a theoretical level, where the methodological validity of the biographical approach is questioned, along with the use of biographies as an interpretative and analytical instrument, the possibility of their use in the analysis of social change, and possible links with anthropology and ethnobiography. Moreover, some essays examine links with daily life and ritual or the imaginary. There are several suggestions for research conducted on this methodical basis. The authors include Paul Thompson, Daniel Bertaux, Michel Maffesoli, Franco Ferrarotti, and Nicole Gagnon.

Hoerning, Erika M. "Biografische Methode in der Sozialforschung." *Das Argument* 22, no. 123 (1980): 667–687.

    The usefulness of the method in the context of qualitative research. The author examines different techniques of data-collection, distinguishing between the idiographic and the nomothetic approach.

Innis, Harold A. *The bias of communication*. (Toronto: University of Toronto Press, 1951).

———. *Empire and Communication*. (Toronto: University of Toronto Press, 1928).

Jelinek, Estelle C., ed. *Woman's Autobiography*. Bloomington: Indiana University Press, 1980.

    A broad excursus, with special reference to Gertrude Stein and Lillian Hellman.

Jobert, Guy. "Entretien avec Franco Ferrarotti." *Education permanente* no. 72–73 (1984): 25–31.

    An interview at the start of the number of Education permanente wholly devoted to life histories and their application to research and training. Among the subjects examined are the methods of collecting biographical accounts, the socio-psychological aspects of life stories, their importance in training and of the autobiography-project.

Joutard, Philippe. *Ces voix qui nous viennent qu passé*. Paris: Hachette, 1983.

    The author rehearses the history of techniques and theories

of oral history in Europe and the United States, stressing most carefully the French experience and his personal intellectual itinerary as a historian for whom the need for collecting oral material sprang directly from his research.

Katz, Elihu and Lazarsfeld, Paul F. *Personal Influence*. Glencoe, Ill.: Free Press, 1955.

Kohli, Martin. "Biographical Research in the German Language Area." Paper 10, *Weltkongress für Soziologie*, Mexico-Berlin, 1982.

Kohli, Martin, and Robert, Günther, eds. *Biographie und soziale Wirklichkeit*, Stuttgart: Metzler, 1984.

A collection of essays touching on various levels of the problematic posed by the collection of autobiographies and the use of such materials in the social sciences: from the reply to the question on the effective contribution of autobiographical documents to the study of specific cases, such as the life of engineers, to the significance of the family in the acquisition of consciousness, and the analysis of specific historical crises, like that of Weimar, as biographical experience. Aside from the editors, the collection represents the following: Heinz Bude, Uta Gerhardt, Fritz Schütze, Gerhard Riemann, Siegfried Heinemeier, Harry Hermanns, Hans-Georg Brose, Nicola Hawkins, Katharina Ley, Jürgen Franzke, Thomas Engelhardt, Rudolf Käs, Matthias Murko, Joachim Matthes.

Kroker, Arthur; Innis, Harold; McLuhan, Marshall; and Grant, George. "Technology and the Canadian Mind." *New World Perspective*, Montreal 1984.

Kröll, Friedhelm. "Biographie? Ein Sozialforschungsweg." *Das Argument* no. 126 (1981): 181–196.

La CS, "Biografia e società a Ginevra." *La critica sociologica* no. 65 (1983): 136–137.

A short summary of a seminar held by F. Ferrarotti at the University of Geneva on life-histories, with development of the implications of the relation between fragment and totality according to some insights by scientists such as I. Prygogine and R. Thom.

Lalive d'Epinay, Christian. "Récit de vie et connaissance scientifique." *Recherches sociologiques* 16, no. 2 (1985): 237–249.

The subtitle significantly says, "Or what to do about subjectivity."

———. "La vie quotidienne. Essai de construction d'un concept sociologique et anthropologique."

A paper presented at the conference Sociologia e antropologia della vita quotidiana, Paris, Centre d'Etude sur l'actuel et le quotidien, 8–9 June 1982.

————. (ed.) "Vie quotidienne et récits de vie." *Revue suisse de sociologie* no. 1 (1983) special number.

In the analysis of one day, d'Epinay identifies two moments of special importance in nature and culture, in the dialectic play between routine and happening.

Lalive d'Epinay, Christian; with Alexander, D.; Clemence, A.; Lazega, E.; and Modak, M. "Popular Culture, Religion and Everyday Life." *Social Compass* 18, no. 4 (1981): 405–424.

This article presents an analysis combining the data of a study based on standardized questionnaires of 1600 people aged between 65 and 80, selected at random, and those of life stories from 140 people chosen from the first sample. The authors construct two ethics of the popular classes: the first that of farmers in a mountain region, centered on the stereotypical and basic assertion "God is God." The second concerns the urban popular class and its nucleus is that of the founding stereotype "life is life."

Lanzardo, Liliana. "Fonti orali e storia della classe operaia: indagini sulla coscienza di classe alla Fiat." *Rivista di storia contemporanea* no. 2 (1981): 255–280.

Laub, John H. *Criminology in the Making: An Oral History*. Evanston: Northwestern University Press, 1983.

Lezega, Emanuel; Modak, Marianne; and Lalive d'Epinay, Christian. "Récits de vie quotidienne et problématique de l'énonciation." *Recherches sociologiques* 13, no. 1–2 (1982): 13–25.

Taking as its base a body of 140 accounts of old age gathered in the Suisse Romande, the authors examine the construction of the account of everyday life. This has the characteristic of promoting discursive behavior composed of interlocutory maneuvers justified by the relation specific to sociological discourse, understanding the latter as a language game. The phrase "everyday life" is taken here as a methodological notion helping to curb accounts where the interlocutor is requested to make himself known and operate procedures explaining himself.

Lefort, François. *Du bidonville a l'expulsion. Itineraire d'un jeune algérien de Nanterre*. Paris: Centre études émigrations méditerranéennes, 1980.

Le Goff, Jacques, ed. *La nuova storia*. Milan: Mondadori, 1980.

A collection of texts representative of the new (in Italy) historiographic trends. The concern is with giving an idea of the new dimensions of historical research and its potential, rather than with logic connection between the various articles.

Lejeune, Philippe. "Autobiographie et histoire sociale au xix siècle." In Delhez-Sarlet, pp. 209–234.

The emergence of individual consciousness from the breakup of the rural world and its imaginary state. The autobiographic need has its roots in the precariousness and instability of the emerging classes.

————. *Je est un autre*. Paris: Seuil, 1980.

The author pursues and deepens his lines of study already precisely laid out in previous works, such as *Le pacte autobiographique* (below), *L'autobiographie en France* (A Colin 1971) *Exercices d'ambiguite* (Lettres Modernes, 1974), *Lire Leiris, autobiographie et language* (Klincksieck, 1975), and is especially concerned with autobiography in its passage from the mainly literary domain to the mass media. He analyzes autobiography from the point of view of the most diverse literary genres, from the account of childhood to the third person autobiography, the radio interview, the guided interview or discussion, the film biography, the autobiographic, documentary and finally the biography told to the anthropological or sociological researcher armed with a recorder. All this appears in the light of Rimbaud's blinding insight: *je est un autre*. Especially profound in his analysis of Sartre's *Les mots*. What is at stake concerns the very idea of "the author." The chapter devoted to the "autobiography of those who do not write," but who are basically the real authors of books, is of great interest in this regard. "They are given the floor, but in reality it is taken away from them to turn the word into writing." The collection of life histories then, according to Lejeune, gives way on the one hand to a new literary genre, and on the other to a new research method in the human sciences. This is not without epistemological and hermeneutical difficulties: "The isolated and developed *récit de vie* is thus an ambiguous object, wavering between science and literature." The way out proposed is not very original: "Technique of correlated life stories allows one to escape the *illusion* of autonomy which each subject tries to preserve, for good or ill, and which the life account tends to accentuate and communicate to the reader" (emphasis in original).

————. *Le pacte autobiographique*. Paris: Seuil, 1975.

The book's slant is essentially literary. Indeed, it is made up
of textual and intertextual analyses of the first book of Rousseau's *Confessions*, and André Gide's *Si le grain ne meurt*,
Sartre's *Les mots*, and the work of Michel Leiris. But the interest for the human sciences is soon revealed when considering the author's basic assumption: "There is a correlation between the development of autobiographical literature and the
rise of a new dominant class, the bourgeoisie, in the same way
that the literary genre of memoirs is closely linked to the evolution of the feudal system."

Levi, Primo. *I sommersi e i salvati*. Turin: Einaudi, 1986.

The book is particularly important for our subject where it
recalls and explores the selective mechanisms of memory and
the processes of degradation that inevitably involve the butch-
ers and their victims.

Levine, Barry D. *Benjy Lopez—A Picaresque Tale of Emigration and
Return*. New York: Basic Books, 1980.

A first-person narrative of the life of someone escaping poverty in Puerto Rico, his homeland, by enrolling in the U.S.
army; after the war he lives for a while in New York, eventually returning to Puerto Rico, where he finally manages to
achieve emotional stability and economic prosperity.

Levy, René. "Per una ricerca biografica integrata." *La critica sociologica* no. 70 (1984): 6–40.

We are reminded of the different approaches to be met with
in France, Germany, and the United States regarding the use
of life-histories, and the proposal to "analyze life histories and
autobiographical reconstructions in a structural-sociological
perspective." The starting point is the analysis of life histories
"primarily if not exclusively as biographies of role and status."
In this perspective, the attention of the author dwells on the
process of aging from the macro- and micro-sociological point
of view.

Lévi-Strauss, Claude. *Lo sguardo da lontano*. Translated by Primo
Levi. Turin: Einaudi, 1984.

Of special interest is the chapter of religion, language and
history, and generally the attempt to compare anthropology,
culture, and science.

McCall, Michael. "The Intersection of Structure and Interaction in
Personal Life Stories." In Denzin, N. K., ed. *Studies in Symbolic Interaction*. Vol. 6. Greenwich, CT: JAI Press, 1984.

Liceo Scientifico Statale Giambattista Morgagni. *Storia del quartiere di Donna Olimpia*. Rome: CISD, 1985.

Here the results of a study conducted through two school years by students and teachers of the Morgagni scientific high school in Rome are presented. This is thus an experience clearly linked to teaching but which has been interesting and worthwhile on the informative level too. The fieldwork led to the formation of a photographic archive. The book offers some theoretical contributions on the supports and suggestions offered by sociology, history, and social history (Piero Zocchi); on the space biographies and biographical materials hold in these disciplines; and also on the different types of language spoken, on the various languages of the imagination and of sound (Marina Thiery). An essay by Bruno Regni reconstructs the history of public contributions for housing, from an urbanistic and architectonic point of view. The volume ends with a long thematic section on the "history and remembrance of Donna Olimpia." Particularly interesting are the sections on games and ganglife, juvenile delinquency, and the reminiscences left by Pasolini. The testimonies are reported directly and organized by subjects. All in all, evidence of the work high schools could usefully undertake, making use of the students' support and providing them at the same time with a series of valid instruments of knowledge.

Lorenzino, Amleto. *Le tendenze della communicazione*. Milan: Sugarco, 1982.

Lukács, Gyorgy, ed. *Pensiero vissuto. Autobiografia in forma di dialogo*. Rome: Riuniti, 1983.

At 85, afflicted by a cancer and conscious of having only a few months to live, Lukács dictated to Istvan Eörsi's recorder his clarifications, filled gaps and made connections on the margins of an autobiographical manuscript. He stated: "In me, everything is the continuation of something. I believe that there are no inorganic elements in my evolution." In reality, trying to come to terms with the numerous criticisms and self-criticisms in the course of a peculiarly tormented existence, the interviewer notes how in Lukács a conservative gnoseology is combined with a left ethic.

Macioti, Maria I. "Gruppo ad hoc sulle storie di vita." *La critica sociologica* no. 63–64 (1982–1983): 242–244.

This is a short presentation of work carried out by the working group of the ISA during the tenth world congress held in Mexico City (16-21 August 1982). In particular, attention is given to the contributions of Aspasia Camargo, Brazil, and Martin Kohli, who analyzed the German-language area contributions.

————. "La Magliana nuova a Roma." *La critica sociologica* no. 68 (1983–1984): 39–80.

These are the first summaries of a study carried out over several years in a peripheral urban area of Roma, marked by speculative building, and where there are nuclei of the middle strata and ex-slum dwellers, mostly coming from Prato Rotondo. The morphology of Magliana is presented over time, from 1971; there follow the testimonies of those involved, especially as regards the ex-slum dwellers and the theme of poverty.

————. "Temi emergenti dalle testimonianze autobiografiche." *La critica sociologica* no. 59 (1981): 84–107.

This is a reading of the biographical materials published at different times by Ferrarotti and his contributors, starting from the thematic trends of origins, type of work and employment, level of education, solidarity, relations with institutions (especially the Church), attitudes, the family and the social roles of the inhabitants of some Roman *borgate* and large urban, peripheral districts.

Macioti, Maria I., ed. *Biografia, storia e società. L'uso delle storie di vita nelle scienze sociali*. Naples: Liguori, 1985.

A reconstruction of the use of the biographical method in Italy from the 1950s to the present opens the book: it gives special attention to cultural anthropology and sociology. There follow mostly theoretical contributions on questions of method, and others linked to psychoanalysis and ethnopsychoanalysis, leading to examples from some field work on specific areas of Rome, or phenomena such as political abstentionism. Two contributions linked to TV programs, where the biographical element and that of everyday life seem basic, close the book.

Maffesoli, Michel. "Le rituel et la vie quotidienne comme fondements des histoires de vie." *Cahiers internationaux de sociologie* no. 69 (1980): 341–349.

A proposal to analyze ritual in that it appears to be the foundation of life-history.

Magli, Ida. *Santa Teresa di Lisieux*. Milan: Rizzoli, 1984.

This is the anthropological analysis of a culture—the feminine culture of the nineteenth century—embodied in its extreme and paradoxical aspects in the biography of a woman society has sanctified, precisely as an unreal expression of the myth, of the social imaginary.

Marcos, Jean-Pierre. "Les aleas de l'autobiographie." *Dialectique* 30 (1980): 18–24.

Marchini, Alvaro. *Comunista o capitalista?* Florence: Vallecchi, 1979.

We have here, in the form of a novel and with a preface by Davide Lajolo, the memoirs of Alvaro Marchini, communist with a celebrated past as partisan, but also a well-known figure as a builder, when wealth made in construction was indicated as a typically capitalist one. These are the everyday memories of his past that arise, the rhythms of work, the war, the resistance, problems in his relations with his wife Anita, a good wife, beyond reproof. "They say of him that he is a good father, beyond criticism in his attachment to the family, to Anita, but not a very good husband. But what, in the human and personal sense, does being a husband mean? No one poses the problem of seeking any kind of justification for Sandro's behavior: the facts speak for themselves, and Anita comes out like a sacrifical victim on the altar of family. . . . She, the faithful wife, the exemplary mother who patiently waits for the husband, who submits to his power, respects and carries out his decisions; makes his house welcoming and educates the children, asks for no extravagances or entertainments." The portrait emerges of a man of the old school, believing in work and day-by-day sacrifices, in view of the "triumph of the cause, the victory of good over evil," fearful of expressing fully his beliefs and states of mind lest he be charged with using rhetoric.

Markiewicz-Lagneau, Janina. *La formation d'une pensée sociologique. La societé polonaise de l'entre-deux-guerres.* Paris: Maison des Sciences de l'Homme, 1982.

The author, tracing a picture of contemporary Polish sociology, brings out the originality of the methodological approach that distinguishes the development of Polish sociology from the early 1920s. The work of Thomas and Znaniecki, which had aroused a widespread discussion among American sociologists, was the start for Poland of a school which to the present has met with growing success, where the use of autobiographies is taken as a base for knowledge of social phenomena. From the 1920s, with the initiative of the Polish Institute for

Sociology (Znaniencki) and then also the Institute of Social
Economics (Zrzywicki), competitions were held to collect autobiographies especially of peasants and workers.

Masutti, Maddalena. *Tornerò tra la gente. Il cammino di una donna
nella chiesa*. Turin: Claudiana, 1986.

The universe of nuns is still rather unknown and the testimonies on it rare. For this reason the autobiographical account given here is of great interest, aside from the sincere
concern that infuses it. This is the journey of a woman from a
peasant background who, in seeking God, decides to enter a
convent, not without meeting incomprehension and hostility
in the world of her origins. A friend of eighteen, stammering
a little, confronts her in the fields: she wants to go into a convent, why? to seek God? but who is God then? "I'll tell you
who God is, the God of the rich . . . God of the priests . . . ,
the powerful. . . . Just, just . . . they call him just, this coward? . . . Where is this coward, where?" She remembers the
boy "tormenting the grass, kneeling before me as if he could
have torn God from the ground. And he was twisting his hands.
As if he would strangle Him."

Nor was the woman to find more understanding in the convent, where she was embroiled in formal rules, the sterility of
human relations, humiliations, and injustices. Again, forced to
leave, after trying to find a secular order to enter, she was to
return to the village, but with the sensation of being "chased
back, as if worn out," "marked for life," isolated. The story
goes beyond a release and self-defense, and poses questions on
a certain kind of institution and the role of woman in the
church.

May, Georges. *L'autobiographie*. Paris: PUF, 1979; 2nd revd. ed., 1984.

At the start the author tries to reply to the "where and when,"
the "who" and "why" of autobiography, though these questions
underlie the whole book. In this context he notes that autobiography seems essentially linked with Western European
individualism, acknowledges an important role for Rousseau's
posthumous works, and asks himself about the foundations of
Christianity and lay humanistic individualism. It is true that
Cato the Elder in the *Origines* boasts of not using a single
proper name; history proceeds with its impersonal majesty, like
a force of nature. He notes again that the autobiographer generally writes at the sunset of his life, even if there are excep-
tions, and that the motivation comes under the sign of apolo-
getics and vendetta, even if there are also testimonies on his

own times as well as intellectual autobiographies and those
taking into account mystical crises and religious itineraries.
Above all, in the second part of the book, the essence is more
literary, with good contributions from the viewpoint of rigorous distinction between autobiography and particularly close
literary genres not to be confused with it.

Mehlman, Jeffrey. *A Structural Study of Autobiography*. Ithaca: Cor-
nell University Press, 1974.

Though mainly interested in literary questions, the book,
which concerns Proust, Leiris, Sartre, and Levi-Strauss, contains remarks on specific structural invariants which the researcher in the human sciences may appreciate in his fieldwork.

Morris, Desmond. *I gesti. Origini e Diffusione*. Milan: Mondadori, 1983.

Musil, Robert. *The Man without Qualities*.Translated by Eithne Wil-
kins and Ernst Kaiser. New York: Coward-McCann, 1953.

Norman, Donald A. *Memoria e attenzione*. Milan: Angeli, 1984.

Olney, James, ed. *Autobiography*. Princeton: Princeton University
Press, 1980.

Ong, Walter J. *Orality and Literacy: The Technologizing of the Word*.
New York: Methuen, 1982.

A masterly essay on the differences, or indeed the real qualitative leap between oral cultures and cultures of the written
word, a leap not to be ascribed to the fact that oral cultures
are primitive but, more simply, to the transformations of consciousness produced by the technology of the word. Writing is
one of these technologies. It is not so completely internalized
that it is mistaken for a form of innate consciousness: the vi-
olinist speaks to us directly, affects our aesthetic sense, as if
his soul spoke directly to our own. We simply forget the violin
is the instrument, the technology, which allows him to communicate with us, and that the violin, like the computer today, has had to be studied for years. Writing, as against orality, has produced new models of thought, which in turn have
made the extraordinary development of culture. This, he as-
sures us, will take place for electronic calculators and computers, and therefore the concerns of the vetero-humanists are
misplaced. His reasoning develops with rich references, which
run from the processes of cognitive psychology to historical
linguistics and sociolinguistics, from the history of the classical age to philosophy, sociology, and cultural anthropology. As
once for writing, so now for printing, revolutionary effects have
occurred on modes of thought and transmitting thought. Equally

disturbing will be the effects of widespread introduction of the computer, as has moreover already been found with TV. The author's optimism is beyond dispute. But it is not unconscious. Suffice it to read the chapter on "Plato, writing and computers," in which he shows, following Havelock, that the whole of Platonic epistemology is unconsciously based on a rejection of the old world of oral culture, warm and mobile, the world of personal interactions represented by the poets he did not want in his Republic. Platonic ideas are silent, immobile, without heat, not interactive but isolated, not inserted in the lively human world but above and beyond it. However, Ong does not pass off crudely the world of oral culture as a primitive one. He simply requires forms of organization of knowledge different and foreign, rather uncongenial, to the mind of one who can read and write.

Passerini, Luisa. *Torini operaia e fascismo. Una storia orale.* Rome-Bari: Laterza, 1984.

Luisa Passerini presents a picture of working-class Turin during the 1920s and 1930s. She warns she has no statistical-representative claims to make, but the testimonies collected are worthily situated "on the background of the results achieved by the historiography of the working class in the fascist period, so as to measure the distance of an ideal representativeness." The story of their lives, freely presented by the protagonists, explores the aspects of family, work, and fascism, at the suggestion of the researcher. Thus we have a specific chapter devoted to the visit to Mirafiori by Mussolini (traditions–facts–symbolic values).

In Passerini's discussion the direct testimonies explore certain subjects, throw light on specific aspects, support lines of interpretation. Indeed, the merit of the text is also that of being an interpretive setting-forth of the testimonies, set in a wider historic context: to some extent the opposite of the refusal to analyze, which some say should accompany the use of oral witnesses.

Passerini, Luisa, ed. *Storia orale. Vita quotidiana e cultura materiale delle classi subalterne.* Turin: Rosenberg and Seller, 1980.

Essays by experts in oral history, such as Thompson and Vigne, discussing the use of autobiographies and oral sources in general as research instruments and techniques.

Pereira De Quieroz, Maria Isaura. *O campesinato brasileiro.* Petropolis: Editoria Vozes, 1976.

The well-known Brazilian researcher and scholar tries to

provide here a global idea of the life of Brazilian peasants. There are excellent observations on the Portuguese survivals in rural Brazilian civilization and as regards the passage from specific studies of peasant districts and villages to average rural life.

Pitkin, Donald S. *The House that Giacomo Built*. Cambridge, England: Cambridge University Press, 1985.

Whereas historically oriented sociologists, like Marzio Barbagli in *Sotto lo stesso tetto* (Bologna: Il Mulino, 1984) seem to try to show that already in the fifteenth century in Italy there were restricted conjugal families, or, as we say today, nuclear families, Pitkin tries to prove with Giacomo's story that the extended family resists industrialization and that relative prosperity does not necessarily involve the fragmentation of the ancient solidarities of the enlarged family in favor of a utilitarian or combative individualism. The thrust of the book is essentially cultural-anthropological, but it deserves commendation for the acuteness of the close observation of the micro-social processes of the everyday in a longitudinal perspective, which allows the reader to notice the dynamic aspects that appear in situations that at first sight seem purely stagnant. The events take place between the end of the last century and the 1960s, and there is also a useful, evocative photographic record.

Plimpton, George, ed. *Writers at Work: The Paris Review Interviews*, 3rd series. New York: Viking Press, 1967. The first and second series, Viking 1957 and 1963, were edited by Malcolm Cowley and Van Wyck Brooks.

Interesting information on the method and style of daily working by various writers, mostly English-speaking, but including Alberto Moravia and Georges Simenon. There are often pungent remarks on relations with publishers and the tension between creativity and the needs of the market.

Poirier, Jean; Clapier-Valladon, Simone; Finger, M.; and Roy, C., eds. *L'approche biographique. Refléxions épistémologiques sur une méthode de recherche*. Nice: 1983.

Popper, Karl. *The Logic of Scientific Discovery*. New York: Basic Books, 1959.

Portelli, Alessandro. *Biografia di una città. Storia e racconto: Terni 1830–1985*. Turin: Einaudi, 1985.

The history of Terni is set out and interpreted, with its passage from agricultural center to industrial city. Oral testimony is adopted as a main instrument, accompanied by written sources used as "support, proof, backing," through individual witnesses in a framework which to some extent becomes choral. Thus for Portelli the theme of this study is "this event of *longue durée*; memory, both intimate and collective located between the event, imagination, and story, between history and subjectivity, narrators and listeners who continually intermingle their roles." The author prefaces the testimonies with an introduction, in which he asks himself about the possibility of a real fidelity to the sources: a fidelity that is concerned not so much with the letter of the document used as its meaning and quality, and at the same time can secure the position and interpretation of the researcher himself. In his words, "Working with oral sources means living with ambivalence." The problems of transcribing the tapes, the montage of the transcriptions, and of the relations between memory and the imaginary are faces, where, too, one follows the game of what might, and should, have happened. Rich and redolent with interest and suggestions, the testimonies, which cover a span of more than 150 years, are presented in chapters with titles that immediately refer one to the literary heritage (for example, "How Green Was My Valley").

The Press—A Neglected Factor in the Economic History of the Twentieth Century. (Oxford: Oxford University Press, 1949).

Raphael, Freddy. "Le travail de la memoire et les limites de l'histoire orale." *Annales, economies, societies, civilisations* 35, no. 1 (1980): 127–145.

Revelli, Nuto. *L'anello forte. La donna: testimonianza di vita contadina.* Turin: Einaudi, 1985.

Ricoeur, Paul. *Temps et recit*, vol. 1. Paris: Seuil, 1983.

The author distinguishes two major categories of tale: the historical and the literary. But in his view even the most rigorous historiography remains narrative, and thus literary. A pity he lacks the good will, or perhaps the humility, to undertake research in the field.

Rinaldi, Giovanni. "Biografia, storia e societá. L'uso delle storie di vita nelle scienze sociali." Rome, 3–5 November 1981, in *Fonti orali* no. 2–3 (1981): 36–38.

The interdisciplinary approach to the subject is stressed, dwelling on the specific space devoted to women, through the examination of audiovisual materials and the feminist press, and there is discussion of oral sources and non-verbal communication in the biographical method. The reference point is

the conference on "Biografia, storia e societa," organized by
the Faculty of Pedagogy, Rome, in November 1981.

Romano, Ruggero, ed. *Le frontiere del tempo*. Milan: Il Saggiatore,
1981.

Rust, Holger. "Qualitative Inhaltsanalyse: Begriffslose Willkür oder
wissenschaftliche Methode? Ein theoretischer Entwurf." *Pub-
lizistik* 25, no. 1 (1980): 5–23.

On the possibility of standardizing techniques of content
analysis in the broader framework of an ethno-anthropological
and linguistic perspective integrating quantitative (structural) data and qualitative descriptions.

Sartre, Jean Paul. *L'idiot de la famille, Gustave Flaubert de 1821 à
1857*. 2 vols. Paris: Gallimard, 1971.

On its first appearance, this monumental contextual biography of Flaubert, as I propose calling it, aroused a storm of
questions. These were times of absolute commitment: the pro-
tests and peremptory chiliastic demands of 1968 were still in
the air. How could the Sartre of 1968 write and publish in
1971 this dusty ponderous tome of pure scholarship on Flaubert, the uncommitted writer par excellence. Tired of commitment or simply needing to refresh himself at the sources of
the myth of literariness? Does Sartre's Flaubert thus reject
the Sartre of *What Is Literature*? A cutting, whether positive
or negative, reply would be too simple not to recall a simplistic
schematism, or do justice to the basic ambiguity which has
always linked the author of *Words* to the author of *Madame
Bovary*. This ambiguity cannot be resolved precisely because
Sartre's undertaking—to read a universe, or a whole society,
in the biography of a single person—is a desperate one. Yet it
must be attempted. Indeed, this involves a real *Grenz-Begriff*,
or idea-limit, the deep intention underlying and justifying the
approach based on life-histories. Sartre's starts from the "con-
stitution" or biogenetic apparatus and the first steps of primary socialization, in this son whose mother, far from recognizing the genius, never even managed to recognize a certain
talent; and who instead was to seem to the whole family, rather
slow, if not retarded or a downright "idiot," slow to walk and
talk. Sartre remarked: "What must be understood is that he
uses words but does not speak. To speak in one way or another, is an act. . . . Gustave, in ecstasy, obsessed by the word,
does not employ holophrastic names or phrases presented; he
does not refuse to use them, that too would always be an act.

Rather, let us say he abandons himself to the force of inertia. You see how he speaks of his poetic insights: *receives* them, it is said" (emphasis in text). It is incredible how Sartre traverses Gustave's infancy, adolescence, and puberty in a constant dialectical relation with the family setting and with the larger extra-familial society, towards personalization. Indeed, "It is necesary that we follow Flaubert in his human relations and his relations with Art. . . . But what we must above all ask ourselves—for this element can be found in every twist of the spiral from the first one—is what the *choice of the unreal* means" (emphasis in text). To Sartre, Flaubert will be able to escape his social class only by putting himself beneath it, "that is, by making himself disqualified and thrown away like an *unusable* instrument" (emphasis in text). And it is when he learns that "the way towards 'superhumanity' passes first from below, alongside the sub-men." In other words, the gift does not exist. Nothing is given. Sartre, theorist of commitment and practical champion of it right to the end, to the editorship of *L'idiot international*, here is theorizing, at the end of his study, on the way to become pure, absolute artists: "One becomes an artist by *conversion*. . . . The *practical* man, even when he devoted all his time to reading good authors and 'making' literature cannot, on principle, be a writer" (emphasis in text). One says *art* to indicate the choice of unreality. From the viewpoint of the wisdom of the practical man, the artist has to convince himself that he is a failure. Neurosis is the price of authenticity.

Sedgwick, Charles P. "The Life History: A Method, with Issues, Troubles and Future." *Working Paper no. 1*, Dept. of Sociology, University of Canterbury, New Zealand, 1980, 1983.

Seppilli, Anita. *La memoria e l'assenza. Tradizione orale e civilta' della scrittura nell'America dei Conquistadores.* Bologna: Cappelli, 1979.

This study concerns material and historical experiences totally foreign to the "Greek world"; however, the author applies logically and acutely the paradox from which E. A. Havelock started to identify the spirit driving Plato. What, before him, did poetry and poems represent in the Greek *paideia*? How is it he excludes them? It is clear that the absence of writing and possession of it condition two forms of thought which are deeply different.

Spengemann, William C. *The Forms of Autobiography*. New Haven: Yale University Press, 1980.

An essentially literary treatment: St. Augustine, Dante, Benjamin Franklin, Thomas de Quincey, Thomas Carlyle.

Starobinski, Jean. *Montaigne en mouvement*. Paris: Gallimard, 1982.
The famous Swiss critic wants to produce a portrait of Montaigne, not a static snapshot, but rather a dynamic portrait, in which he intends to identify and then describe the successive stages of a thought that derives its impetus from an act of refusal. This is not Montaigne's movement as it has usually been understood and explained. The movement the author's study refers to is that which inspires the logical consequences of the initial negation. This negation is at the same time a thought, a logico-theoretical act, and an existential decision that practically ends Montaigne's political career. But the author is well aware that Montaigne himself had put his interpreters on guard when he warned that "it is harder to interpret interpretations than interpret things." In fact, the author discovers that Montaigne is the aim, none other than himself, of Montaigne's writing. With him we face the pure autobiographical act. St. Augustine, through the autobiographical retroactive glance, sought dialogue with God; Rousseau remains, in the scandal of absolute sincerity, a pedagogue moved by direct and indirect edifying intentions. Montaigne observes himself; he has no ends external to the act of self-observation; he aims at nothing else. Suspicion surrounds him. Doubt leaves him no safety margin. There remain bodily sensations, life in its narrow but real limits, potentially capable of fullness. Not the science of life, but rather, life: "In place of the arts which make life their *object* and pretend to govern it, he sets life itself, which he experiences directly—life raised to the level of art" (emphasis in text). Indeed, he writes "My trade and my art is living." Starobinski remarks, "The singular subject frees himself from the general discussion concerning him and claims for himself, alone, the *authority* of knowing, of a radically different knowledge, which we know he almost confused with feeling" (emphasis in text). In seven chapters, Starobinski examines the main themes of Montaigne's dynamic meditation: friendship, death, freedom, the body, love, language, and public life.

Steinauer, J. *Le saisonnier inexistant*. Geneva: Editions Que faire?, 1980.

Stone, Albert E. *Autobiographical Occasions and Original Acts*, Philadelphia: University of Pennsylvania Press, 1982.
Stone's effort lies in tracing the links and problematic tran-

sitions between individual histories and "cultural narratives." Autobiography is seen as an original act in Starobinski's sense, or insofar as it links the self to his past in the light of his present.

Thomas, William I. and Znaniecki, Florian. *The Polish Peasant in Europe and America.* Chicago: The University of Chicago Press, 1918–1920.

Thompson, Paul. "Des récits de vie à l'analyse du changement social." *Cahiers internationaux de sociologie* no. 69 (1980): 249–268.

According to the author, social historians, especially "oral" ones, and sociologists involved in gathering life-histories, are fated to meet. Thus there could arise a new outlook in social research, which Thompson calls "ethno-history," that could contribute to a better understanding of social change and its actors.

Thompson, Paul, ed. *Our Common History: The Transformation of Europe.* Highlands, NJ: Humanities Press, Atlantic, 1982.

Nineteenth-century European history reconstructed by way of collections of oral history and reflections on the most significant moments of our collective memory.

Tolton, C.D.E. *André Gide and the Art of Autobiography.* Toronto: Macmillan, 1975.

The author dwells on and clarifies Gide's distinction between *recit, sotie,* and *roman.* The object of a textual analysis, carried out also on the original manuscript, is Gide's autobiographical work *Si le grain ne meurt* (If it die).

Turner, William H., and Cabbell, Edward J., eds. *Blacks in Appalachia.* Lexington: University Press of Kentucky, 1985.

An exemplary essay on history and sociology "from below."

Ulivi, Loredana. *Isola del Giglio. Una comunitá in transizione.* Roma: Bulzoni, 1984.

Zocchi, Piero, and Mayer, Giovanni. "A proposito di una recente ricerca condotta con il metodo delle storie di vita." *La critica sociologica* no. 60 (1981–1982): 142–146.

These are two contributions regarding *Storie senza storie* by Renato Cavallaro, where Cavallaro's proposed linguistic analysis of the evidence is examined along with the mode of transcription used—literal and orthographic. Especially discussed is the presentation of social stratification, the not always sufficiently pronounced development of the conflictual element, the dynamic elements, and those of potential rupture of a preceding equilibrium.

Zonabend, Francoise. La *"memoria lunga." I giorni della storia.* Rome: Armando, 1985.

Zucconi, Angela. *Autobiografia di un paese.* Milan: Ed. di Comunitá, 1984.

The history of a little commune in Latium from Unity to fascism, basically reconstructed through the use of material kept in the communal archive at Anguillara, and complemented for specific aspects by other sources, such as the parish archive, private documents, etc. Among the sources chosen, the author warns that the most "voluble" ones have been selected, "like medical reports, the public school teachers, sentences from the mediators, police and gamekeepers' reports, letters to the mayor, petitions, etc." This is thus a method not new to some types of history, with the advantage of bringing to light facts and expectations, precisely reconstructed, also aware of the need to expand its own limits: from the voluble papers one can thus find an opening to oral sources, even if the use of these is still an auxiliary, complementary one, in a discussion essentially built on secondary sources.

Index

About the Author

FRANCO FERRAROTTI is Professor of Sociology and Chairman of the Ph.D. Program in Social Science at the University of Rome, Italy. He is the author of *The Myth of Inevitable Progress* and *Five Scenarios for the Year 2000* (Greenwood Press, 1985, 1986), as well as *Toward The Social Production of the Sacred, Alternative Sociology, Max Weber and the Destiny of Reason, Max Weber and the Crisis of Western Civilization,* and *A Theology for Non-Believers.* His articles have appeared in numerous publications, including *Social Research, State, Culture, and Society,* and *La Critica Sociologica.*